The WW
Essential Guide to
Healthy Eating

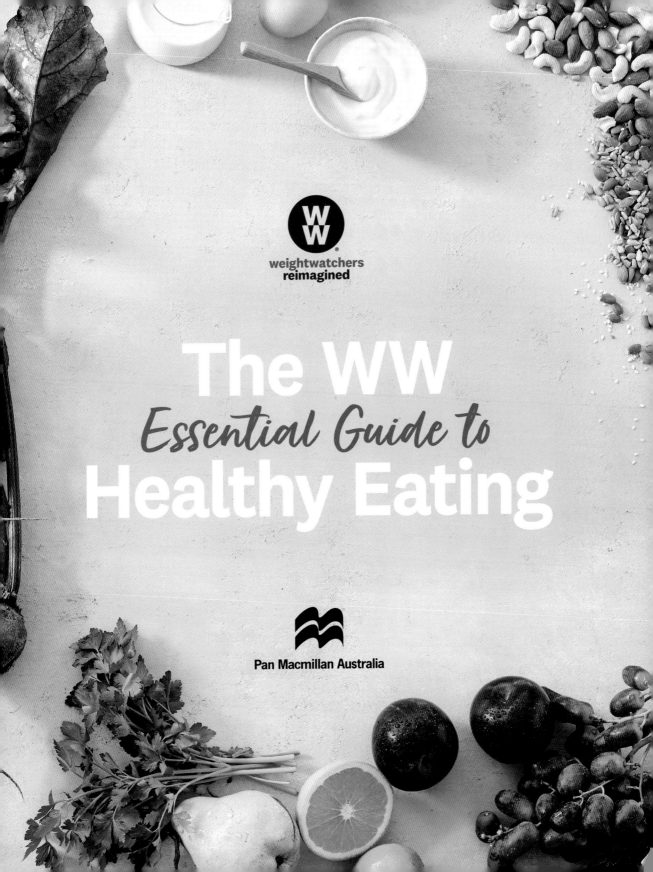

The WW
Essential Guide to
Healthy Eating

Pan Macmillan Australia

Contents

PART ONE

The WW way

Welcome to WW

weightwatchers
reimagined

From humble beginnings to the world's leading sustainable weight-loss program with over 5 million members, WW (formerly known as Weight Watchers) has come a long way since it all started more than 55 years ago, evolving from one woman's inspiring success story to that of many.

WHERE IT ALL BEGAN

Jean Nidetch, the company founder, had been overweight most of her life. She had become discouraged by years of fad dieting, having tried pills, hypnosis and numerous quick-fix approaches, all of which led to regained weight. She decided to seek medically backed guidance instead, and entered a free 10-week weight-loss program called the 'Prudent Diet', sponsored by the New York City Board of Health's obesity clinic. She lost 9 kg, but her motivation waned with the lack of peer support she had received during the program. This is when Jean's weekly meetings with her own support group began, and the seed for Weight Watchers was planted.

Jean began her own weight-loss support group by inviting some of her friends to her home once a week to discuss their goals, tips and challenges for weight-loss success. As word spread and attendee numbers grew, she finally launched Weight Watchers Inc. in May 1963. The first official meeting, held in a rented loft above a movie theatre in Queens, New York, attracted more than 400 attendees. The winning formula of Weight Watchers quickly spread across the world and to Australia in 1969, where the first meeting was held in Sydney.

WHAT WE DO TODAY

In 2018, Weight Watchers became WW, reflecting our evolution into what we are today: a wellness company powered by the world's leading sustainable weight-loss program. Having constantly evolved in line with the latest science and member needs, we've stood the test of time, delivering a trusted program that remains a category leader both in Australia and across the globe. WW has retained the number-one spot for weight loss for 10 consecutive years, as judged by an independent panel of experts in the US News & World Report. It's also backed by more than 100 clinical studies and is supported by even more incredible member success stories.

At WW, our purpose is to inspire healthy habits for real life. While supporting members at physical locations and virtual workshops, we have also built a digital experience centred on the award-winning WW app that allows people to learn healthy habits their way. In addition to food, fitness, sleep and water tracking, the WW app includes everything from recipes and 24/7 WW Coach support, to a barcode scanner, meditations, and audio and video workouts, providing support across the pillars of food, movement and mindset (see page 10).

COMMUNITY AT OUR CORE

Community remains at the heart of our philosophy and it is this community that differentiates us in the market. Our network of Coaches, Ambassadors and Members live our purpose daily, encouraging and supporting each other through our community platforms to pay forward the techniques and success they've achieved with others. We are incredibly proud of our Members' achievements and even more so of their ability to make these changes lasting and sustainable.

What's that symbol?

Our guide to finding the best recipes for your dietary needs

Gluten free Recipes with this symbol either don't contain any gluten or a gluten-free substitute is available. Check the ingredients list of all packaged food to be sure and take care with cross-contamination.

Dairy free Recipes with this symbol are free from all dairy products or use a dairy-free substitute.

Vegetarian Recipes with this symbol don't contain meat or fish, but may have dairy products or eggs.

Vegan Recipes with this symbol don't contain any animal products, including meat, dairy, eggs and other animal-derived substances.

Nut free Recipes with this symbol don't contain any nuts or nut-based products. Check the ingredients list of all packaged food to be sure and take care with cross-contamination.

Please note: the recipes in this book have been reviewed by our team of qualified nutritionists to ensure that the information listed is as accurate as possible. However, people with food allergies or sensitivities should always check the ingredient information of the products they consume to ensure that they meet their dietary needs.

The 3 pillars

The WW program takes a holistic approach to weight loss and wellness, based on 3 pillars: food, movement and mindset.

1 FOOD

One of the benefits of WW is that we support you in discovering how to cook and enjoy healthier meals that suit your individual lifestyle. This can help you to develop eating habits that will stay with you long after you reach your goals. You don't have to be a chef to enjoy healthy, delicious meals. With our helpful eating tips, you'll be on your way to creating healthy habits!

Make an effort to plan ahead. WW is all about flexibility and choice so you don't have to plan everything that you eat in detail in order to be successful. However, planning some of your meals will help you make healthier choices. Spend some time on the weekend planning the recipes you want to cook and eat that week. Then, when you do your grocery shop, write a list and stick to it, and try not to be persuaded by less healthy options available in the moment.

Enjoy more fruit and vegetables. Fruit and vegetables are great options for when you're feeling peckish or you want to bulk up your meal. Build the habit of filling half your plate with non-starchy vegetables and choose 2 serves of fruit to enjoy throughout the day. Mix things up as much as you can as different fruit and vegies have different nutrients. Colour is a great indicator of this, so try to eat a rainbow each day.

Eat plenty of wholefoods. When we talk about wholefoods, we mean food that is less processed and is as close to nature as possible (think fresh fruit and vegetables; fresh meat, chicken and seafood; fresh milk; legumes; and whole grains such as brown rice and barley). They can be better for your health as they offer more nutrients and fibre, and often take longer to digest (meaning you'll feel fuller for longer).

Embrace home-cooked meals. One of the best ways to achieve your health and wellness goals is to cook at home regularly. This way, you can control the type of ingredients, cooking methods and portion sizes, as well as track what you're eating, accurately. Home cooking can also help you de-stress after a busy day, eat more mindfully and nurture family bonds if you get them involved in the process.

Try something new. Be open to eating fresh ingredients that you may not normally put in your trolley. Pick up that unusual vegetable or if you haven't eaten something since you were a child, try it again – you never know, you may like it! An easy way to do this is to cook one new recipe a week. If you enjoy it, add it to your regular meals. If you don't, move on and try a new one next week. Trying new things makes meal times more exciting and helps keep you motivated.

2 MOVEMENT

At WW, being active is about moving more, no matter how you do it. Anything that gets you off the sofa more will greatly benefit your health, mood and wellbeing.

Start today. Start small. Walking is a great activity to build on. We recommend you begin with 10 minutes of low-intensity exercise 3 days a week and build up to 30 minutes of moderate-intensity exercise 5 days a week.

Find something you enjoy doing. If you have fun being active, you're more likely to stick with it long term. Shift your mindset from working out for 'exercise' to working out for 'fun'. When you do something you love that just happens to be active, rather than pushing yourself to do types of exercise you don't really enjoy, you're likely to feel happier and less daunted by your workouts.

Do more incidental activity. It's a common misconception that being physically active requires going to a gym or splashing out on expensive equipment. The fact is many everyday activities, from gardening to walking your dog, count as valuable activity. The key is to embrace the concept of seeing all movement as an opportunity, not an inconvenience.

Set achievable goals. You're more likely to keep at something if you set and achieve realistic goals along the way. Research shows that tracking your activity and sticking to your goals can also increase the amount of exercise you do.

Make it a priority. It's time to start putting yourself first – at least sometimes. This includes finding time for activity, even if it's just a few minutes here and there to begin with. Grab every opportunity to stand rather than sit, and make it your mission to take more steps each day using a combination of planned and incidental activity.

3 MINDSET

A fundamental part of the WW program is learning how to shift your mindset to a more helpful state so you can make different choices that align better with your goals. Science tells us that what you *think* determines how you *feel* and how you feel determines what you *do*. Having a more positive outlook can make you better equipped to solve problems and handle stress.

Appreciate positive things. This can be something as small as appreciating a good cup of coffee. Paying attention to the small things and being thankful for them boosts wellbeing.

Celebrate little wins. We're all prone to waiting for 'big' moments to make us happy. Reflect on the wonderful little things that are already happening right now.

Counter negative self-talk. If you catch yourself criticising your body or abilities, counter the impulse with positive responses.

Go easy on yourself. While setting goals can help put you on a productive path, overarching expectations can lead to feelings of failure that foster negativity. To remain realistic, make sure your goals are actionable. Once you decide what you'd like to accomplish, determine what you'll do to get there plus when you'll do it, where and with whom (if anyone).

Connect with others. Whether it's cosying up on the couch with your partner or scheduling a happy hour with your friends, spending time with people who make you feel good is a sure-fire way to improve your outlook.

Visualise your best possible self. What does life look like if everything goes as well as it could – in 1, 5 and 10 years' time? How do you feel? Mental imagery can help you keep your sights on your values and inspire you to go for it.

How myWW works

The program from WW is now customised to your needs, making losing weight easier than ever! Using a personal assessment of your food preferences and lifestyle in the WW app, *myWW* matches you to one of three food plans that best suits you – Green, Blue or Purple.

SMARTPOINTS

On all three plans, every food and drink is assigned a SmartPoints® value. You're given a daily SmartPoints budget based on your age, gender, weight and height, and you can choose to spend it on any foods or drinks you like (which means you don't have to say no to a glass of wine with dinner or a chocolate treat occassionally!). No food is off-limits on WW, so you don't need to miss out on the foods you love.

ZEROPOINT FOODS

There's also an extensive list of ZeroPoint™ foods on every plan, containing options that form the foundations for healthy eating patterns, which don't need to be measured or tracked. Depending on which plan you follow, these foods range from fruit and vegetables through to seafood, skinless chicken breast and even whole grain pasta.

FITPOINTS

You'll also get a personalised FitPoints® goal to motivate you to move more. FitPoints are similar to SmartPoints but instead of tracking food, they help you track activity. FitPoints take into account your height, weight, age and gender, as well as activity type and duration, to calculate a personalised FitPoints value for all of the activities you do. You earn FitPoints for any steps you take and any activity you do, plus it nudges you towards better-for-you activities including high intensity and strength training.

All WW Members have access to our award-winning app which allows you to take the program with you wherever you go. Track your SmartPoints, weight and activity, follow guided meditations and workouts, and chat to a WW Coach 24/7.

WHAT CAN YOU DO IN THE WW APP?

* **Simple food and fitness tracking.** Your dashboard is your home base for tracking.
* **Browse 5,000+ recipes.** Search recipes by selecting a category, then apply filters such as SmartPoints value. You can customise any WW recipe by hitting the edit button. Tweak it and save it as your own. You can also build your own recipes and meals and save them to your favourites library for easy reference. The SmartPoints value will display whichever food plan you are following (Green, Blue or Purple).
* **Track your water.** A new feature allows you to track how much water you're drinking.

* **Track your sleep.** Now you can track your sleep, just like you track food and activity! The app also includes a science-backed technique to help you enjoy a little more shut-eye.

* **Food barcode scanner.** Once you've scanned a food or drink, you can save it, add it to your favourites and track it. This handy tool makes it helpful to compare items at the supermarket to help you make the healthier choice.

* **Weight loss and journey tracker.** Log your weekly weight (or sync your smart scales to automatically track for you) and view your progress graphs and reflections.

* **Meditate with Headspace.** At WW, we know that how you think drives the things you do. One of the ways to make a positive shift is meditation. That's why we've partnered with Headspace, a leader in meditation and mindfulness, to help you meditate any time, anywhere.

* **Video workouts with FitOn.** We've partnered with FitOn to create exclusive workouts. There's something for everyone, no matter what your current fitness level is.

* **Audio-based workouts with Aaptiv.** We've also partnered with Aaptiv to give you even more ways to workout right from the WW app.

* **Member social community.** Connect is our social community for members. It's a positive and inspirational space where you can make new friends. Share your photos and progress and follow other members on their journeys. It's the best place to hang out for a motivation boost! And with Connect Groups, you can get support from like-minded members including groups for each food plan colour.

* **Live chat with a WW Coach.** Whether you need advice, motivation or tech help, our expert WW Coaches are online 24/7. Click on the Help tab to instantly chat with an expert whenever you need them.

Top tips for achieving sustainable weight loss

Dr Michelle Celander, Director of Program and Food Content at WW in Australia and New Zealand, shares her top tips for successful long-term weight loss.

1 SET REALISTIC WEIGHT-LOSS GOALS, AS WELL AS SHORT-TERM BEHAVIOURAL GOALS ALONG YOUR JOURNEY

This will help you stay motivated and focused on what you need to do in order to achieve your long-term health and weight-loss goals.

2 DON'T RESTRICT OR CUT OUT WHOLE FOOD GROUPS

Sustainable weight loss is not about cutting out the foods you enjoy, it's about learning how to integrate them in a healthier way. Cutting out whole food groups means you may start lacking essential nutrients and studies show you end up wanting these foods even more if you try to cut them out completely.

3 MANAGE YOUR PORTIONS

Try to reduce the portion sizes of higher-energy foods and load up on vegies and lean proteins. Sustainable weight loss is all about making small changes to your eating that still fit in with your lifestyle. For example, adding an extra serve of vegetables to your main meals or drinking one glass of wine with dinner rather than two or three. It's these small steps that make a big difference in the long run.

4 FOCUS ON BUILDING HEALTHY HABITS

Research shows it's much more effective to focus on starting new healthy habits rather than trying to stop unhealthy habits. For example instead of cutting out eating biscuits with a cup of tea in the afternoon, focus on starting to eat a piece of fruit with your tea instead. This will help form a new healthier habit loop which associates drinking your afternoon tea with eating a piece of fruit.

5 SET UP A NETWORK OF SOCIAL SUPPORT

Studies show people with social support are more likely to engage in healthy eating and physical activity behaviours. They're also better able to cope with stressful events which can be a derailer for some people when trying to lose weight. Surround yourself with people who offer words of encouragement and motivate you to keep going through challenging times.

6 MOVE MORE IN WAYS YOU ENJOY

Activity plays an important part in improving your overall health, as well as helping you achieve your weight-loss goals. What's most important when it comes to regular activity is finding something you enjoy doing. You're more likely to stick with something if you find it fun.

7 LISTEN TO YOUR HUNGER AND FULLNESS SIGNALS

Learning how to eat more mindfully (chewing slowly, taking breaks between mouthfuls, eating without distractions like the TV or phone) will help you start to listen to your body and stop eating once you're full. It's also important to learn the difference between internal and external hunger. Internal hunger is when you are genuinely hungry, often you haven't eaten for a few hours and any type of food will be satisfying. External hunger comes on suddenly and is usually due to the smell or sight of a certain food, such as hot chips or leftover cake in the office. Knowing the difference between the two types of hunger can help set you up for long-term weight-loss success.

8 CELEBRATE SMALL WINS

Celebrate every small step you take towards achieving your goals. It's important to give yourself recognition for the efforts you've made along your journey, not just once you've reached your goal. This will help you stay motivated when you need it most.

Meet Michelle

Dr Celander is a qualified dietitian and research scientist, responsible for ensuring the integrity of the WW program and the accuracy of all content created for members. While most of her career has been spent leading nutrition teams in food companies across the globe, her 17 years' experience also spans clinical practice, university lecturing, health communications, regulatory affairs and nutrition research. Michelle is passionate about earning trust through translating credible science into compelling communication and truly helping people reach their health goals.

WW Member story: *Irene Morton*

'THAT' AWKWARD QUESTION

Weighing close to 110 kg, Irene kept being asked if she was pregnant. 'People would say, "Are you having —", and I'd cut them off, saying, "Don't finish that sentence!"' said the 35-year-old mother of three. The hurtful questions weren't the only factors that led to her addressing her weight. 'When I couldn't do up my shoes as easily as I should, I knew something had to change.'

FOCUSED FROM DAY ONE

Since walking through the WW doors, Irene has been determined to reach her Goal of 76 kg. 'I focused on myself and realised my weight was something I could concentrate on,' she says. 'Some things in life are uncontrollable, but your weight isn't one of them and with that control, you feel empowered. I'd tried many weight-loss options before but depriving myself led to binge eating, and cutting out carbs gave me headaches. With WW, you don't have to pop diet pills or drink silly shakes. It has shown me how to change my cooking and it has educated me on eating well. It's taught me how to lead a healthy lifestyle.'

MOTIVATION AND TEMPTATION

Irene's vigilance on the program has meant she hasn't gained weight once in the first six months of her journey, but that's not to say it's all been smooth sailing. Whenever Irene feels less than motivated, she looks back – literally.

'I look at old photos of myself that I keep on my phone and I never want to look like that again,' she says. 'Doing this always helps me move forward.'

Social occasions have tested her, too, such as her mum's recent birthday. 'I ate and drank more than I should have, but these events will come up. After a celebration like that I'm more mindful of what I eat,' she says. 'That's the beauty of the WW program. All of those ZeroPoint foods make it easier to stick to my SmartPoints Budget.'

TRACKING LEADS TO SUCCESS

The flexibility of the program goes beyond big social events; dinner out with the family is easier, too. 'There are so many options when we go out,' says Irene. 'If I want chicken, I'll choose the breast over schnitzel and still have chips with salad on the side. If you've gone over your Points, you don't have to starve – you can still eat a big salad with lean proteins and be fine.'

'Eat it, track it' has been Irene's mantra from the get-go. 'A bite of a doughnut here, a crust of bread there … it all equates to something!' she says. 'If I've had a small bite of a doughnut, I work out the SmartPoints of how much I've had and track it. A nibble could be 2 SmartPoints.'

Irene also uses her kitchen scales. 'I weigh 90 per cent of what I eat – the scales live on my kitchen bench. I can narrow everything down to the exact SmartPoint.'

SWAPPING RATHER THAN STOPPING

While Irene has kicked some habits – such as soft drinks – for the most part, she's made compromises. 'I have a square or two of chocolate every day,' she says. 'I put the block straight back into the fridge and walk away. I've learned self-control.' Her catchphrase is 'I haven't stopped – I've swapped'. 'For example, when it's hot weather and I feel like a slushie, I get one that has less than 1 per cent sugar.'

LIKE MOTHER, LIKE DAUGHTER

Irene and her mum have been on WW together, with her mum losing 24 kg so far. 'We keep each other going,' says Irene. 'She wouldn't have done it without me, and I may have given up if it wasn't for her. The support works well in my moments of madness. Mum will ask, "Irene, is it worth it?"'

Irene's kids – Ashton, Alexsis and Layton – have also been her inspiration. 'My little girl comes up to me now and comments that her two hands can touch when she wraps her arms around me,' says Irene. 'I'm having more fun and we bond over the simplest things. I do cartwheels in the backyard and get down on the ground and jump up like a jack-in-the-box.'

Irene says that she has a renewed sense of purpose. 'I was never unhappy before but, as cheesy as it sounds, I've learned to love myself and have found the true meaning of happiness.'

> 'Some things in life are uncontrollable, but your weight isn't one of them and with that control, you feel empowered.'

Then

Now

WHAT I LOVE ABOUT WW

1 There are so many ZeroPoint foods that I love, such as eggs and chicken breast on the blue and purple food plan, which make my meals lower in Points.

2 It's given me a new look on life. It isn't the second phase of a diet, it's a lifestyle I love!

3 You get to have your cake and eat it, too! You can enjoy the sweeter things in life and not have to stress about it.

4 I love that I can indulge on weekends and still eat real food throughout the week. I don't miss out on anything and can have whatever I want so long as I have the Points for it.

*Irene lost weight on prior WW program and continued on *myWW*. Weight loss may vary.

Successful shopping

Sticking to a list that you've prepared can help to reduce the likelihood of impulse purchases at the shops. Try to avoid shopping on an empty stomach, too. When you're hungry, you're likely to buy more than you need.

Shop in season

Buying what's in season rather than just what's on offer has some serious benefits, from reducing your grocery bill to minimising your environmental footprint. If you're not yet a convert of buying in season, these perks may just change your mind.

COST

The abundance of in-season produce and minimal transportation costs generally means that prices are pushed down. Out-of-season produce is often transported long distances and refrigerated for lengthy periods of time which drives up the cost.

TASTE

If you've ever eaten a tomato straight off the vine or a freshly picked strawberry, you'll know how amazing fresh fruit and vegetables can taste. The flavour of out-of-season produce just doesn't compare. When fruit and vegetables are stored for long periods before being sold, they're usually harvested before they're ripe, resulting in a less intense flavour.

NUTRITION

While all fresh produce is nutritious, seasonal produce is often much higher in nutrients. As fruit and vegetables ripen, their nutrient levels increase accordingly, so eating them at peak ripeness not only means they taste better, you get maximum nutrition benefits, too. Eating seasonally also means we eat a greater variety of foods, as our diet naturally changes with the seasons, rather than buying the same items out of habit. And of course, a greater variety on our plates means a greater range of nutrients for our bodies to benefit from.

ENVIRONMENTAL IMPACT

Buying seasonally not only supports local farmers, it's also better for the planet as it reduces the need for hot houses and refrigeration, and reduces 'food miles' (the distance our food travels to get to us), all of which contribute to pollution and add to our environmental footprint.

Top tips for the trolley

❋ **Perfect produce** Stock up on onions, apples, pumpkin, carrots, beetroot, cabbage, citrus fruit and celery. They're ZeroPoint foods and have some of the longest shelf life of all fruit and vegies.

❋ **Fab frozen** Typically frozen at peak condition, frozen seafood is a convenient source of protein. For safe eating, thaw in the fridge overnight.

❋ **Hearty herbs** The strong flavours of woody herbs, such as thyme and rosemary, are good for cooking, while the more subtle flavours and textures of soft herbs, such as basil, coriander and flat-leaf parsley, are great for adding to salads or scattering over meals for a flavour boost.

Pantry staples

Stock your pantry with these handy staples to help you make healthier choices every day. See page 34 for our tips on organising your pantry.

PANTRY

- [ ] Beans, peas and lentils, canned
- [ ] Capers in vinegar
- [ ] Curry pastes
- [ ] Fruit, canned in natural juice
- [ ] Olive oil spray or extra-virgin olive oil
- [ ] Pasta sauce
- [ ] Pesto
- [ ] Rice, brown
- [ ] Snacks (see page 28)
- [ ] Soup, reduced-salt
- [ ] Stock, reduced-salt chicken or vegetable
- [ ] Tomatoes, canned
- [ ] Tuna or salmon, canned in spring water
- [ ] Vegetables, canned

SEASONINGS & CONDIMENTS

- [ ] Dried herbs and spices, seasoning mixes and dry rubs
- [ ] Salad dressings, fat-free or low-fat
- [ ] Mayonnaise, fat-free or low-fat
- [ ] Mustard
- [ ] Salt and pepper
- [ ] Soy sauce, reduced-salt
- [ ] Vinegar

Fruit *and* veg

Adding lots of vegies to meals is the key to feeling satisfied while losing weight. Packed with vitamins, minerals and fibre, they are great for your health and most are Zero SmartPoints.

Below is a list of our top ingredients to try.

VEGETABLES

- [ ] Alfalfa sprouts
- [ ] Artichoke
- [ ] Asparagus
- [ ] Baby corn
- [ ] Beans
- [ ] Beetroot
- [ ] Bok choy
- [ ] Broad beans
- [ ] Broccoli
- [ ] Broccolini
- [ ] Brussels sprouts
- [ ] Cabbage
- [ ] Capsicum
- [ ] Carrot
- [ ] Cassava
- [ ] Cauliflower
- [ ] Celeriac
- [ ] Celery
- [ ] Chillies
- [ ] Choko
- [ ] Choy sum

- [ ] Corn
- [ ] Cucumber
- [ ] Eggplant
- [ ] Endive
- [ ] Fennel
- [ ] Gai lan (Chinese broccoli)
- [ ] Garlic
- [ ] Golden shallots
- [ ] Kale
- [ ] Leek
- [ ] Lettuce
- [ ] Mushroom
- [ ] Okra
- [ ] Onion
- [ ] Pak choy
- [ ] Parsnips
- [ ] Peas
- [ ] Potato
- [ ] Pumpkin
- [ ] Radicchio

- [ ] Radish
- [ ] Rocket
- [ ] Shallots (spring onions)
- [ ] Silverbeet
- [ ] Snow peas
- [ ] Spinach
- [ ] Squash
- [ ] Sugar snap peas
- [ ] Swede
- [ ] Sweet potato
- [ ] Taro
- [ ] Tomato
- [ ] Turnip
- [ ] Watercress
- [ ] Wombok (Chinese cabbage)
- [ ] Zucchini

FRUIT

- [ ] Apples
- [ ] Apricots
- [ ] Bananas
- [ ] Cherries
- [ ] Blueberries
- [ ] Grapes
- [ ] Kiwifruit
- [ ] Lemon
- [ ] Lime
- [ ] Mandarins
- [ ] Mangoes
- [ ] Nectarines
- [ ] Oranges
- [ ] Peaches
- [ ] Pears
- [ ] Pineapple
- [ ] Plums
- [ ] Raspberries
- [ ] Rockmelon
- [ ] Strawberries
- [ ] Watermelon

Eat a rainbow

Different-coloured fruit and vegies offer different nutrients so try to eat a variety every day.

✻ **Green produce (such as broccoli, beans, spinach, kale and kiwifruit):** Rich in vitamins A and C for healthy skin, iron for red blood cell production, calcium for strong bones, lutein and zeaxanthin (antioxidants) and sulforaphane (a phytonutrient).

✻ **Red produce (such as capsicums, strawberries and tomatoes):** Contains vitamin C to boost immunity, folate for cell function and lycopene (an antioxidant).

✻ **Orange/yellow produce (such as pumpkins, carrots, sweet potatoes and apricots):** Brimming with vitamin C, potassium and beta-carotene (an antioxidant).

✻ **Purple/blue produce (such as blueberries, eggplants, beetroot and purple cabbage):** Provides vitamin C, manganese, plus anthocyanins (antioxidants).

✻ **White produce (such as onions, garlic, mushrooms and cauliflower):** Various B vitamins plus vitamin C.

Legumes *and* grains

Legumes and grains are versatile ingredients that can be used in both sweet and savoury dishes. Enjoy these high-fibre, low-GI options to feel fuller for longer.

Below is a list of our top ingredients to try.

- ☐ Barley
- ☐ Black beans
- ☐ Buckwheat
- ☐ Bulgur
- ☐ Butter beans
- ☐ Cannellini beans
- ☐ Cereals, whole grains
- ☐ Chickpeas
- ☐ Couscous
- ☐ Egg noodles
- ☐ Farro
- ☐ Kidney beans
- ☐ Lentils
- ☐ Oats
- ☐ Pasta
- ☐ Pearl barley
- ☐ Polenta
- ☐ Quinoa
- ☐ Rice, brown
- ☐ Rice noodles
- ☐ Wheat noodles

Dairy, eggs, meat, fish *and* tofu

Protein-rich foods like eggs, meat and dairy are all great hunger-busters. Try to include a source of protein at every meal and snack to ensure you keep hunger at bay.

Below is a list of our top ingredients to try.

MEAT, FISH & TOFU

- [ ] Chicken breast and turkey breast, skinless
- [ ] Beef sirloin steak, lean
- [ ] Minced beef, lean
- [ ] Pork fillet, lean
- [ ] White fish and salmon fillets, fresh or frozen
- [ ] Prawns and shellfish, fresh or frozen
- [ ] Tofu, firm or silken

DAIRY & EGGS

- [ ] Cheese, low-fat or reduced-fat (shredded, cottage, ricotta)
- [ ] Milk, skim or low-fat
- [ ] Yoghurt, 99% fat-free plain
- [ ] Eggs

Snacks

A tasty between-meal snack or occasional dessert can often be a smart choice. They can stop you feeling hungry before your next meal and prove you don't have to deny yourself treats when you're losing weight. So feel free to have them when you need to – it's about balance!

- [ ] Air-popped popcorn
- [ ] Boiled egg
- [ ] Dips, reduced-fat (such as hummus and tzatziki)
- [ ] Dried fruit (such as pitted dates, dried apricots and cranberries)
- [ ] Dry-roasted chickpeas
- [ ] Fruit, fresh and canned in natural juice
- [ ] Miso or non-creamy packet soup
- [ ] Skim-milk cappuccino
- [ ] Tomato salsa
- [ ] Nuts, raw and unsalted (such as almonds, Brazil nuts and walnuts)
- [ ] Vegie sticks
- [ ] Water-based ice-blocks
- [ ] Wholemeal rice cakes or rice crackers
- [ ] WW sweet and savoury snacks (protein bars and balls, rice nibblies, fava beans, chickpea chips, chocolate crisp bars, mini biscuits)
- [ ] Yoghurt, 99% fat-free plain

Track *those* snacks!

Many snacks can be included in your daily meal plans, while your weekly SmartPoints budget is designed for those days when you might need a little bit extra for that special celebration. Here are some of our top tips when it comes to snacking.

DRINK FIRST, EAT LATER

If you're feeling hungry, try drinking a glass of water or herbal tea first and wait for 10 minutes. It could be that you've mistaken thirst for hunger. If you're still feeling hungry after that, grab a snack that fits within your SmartPoints budget to tide you over so you're not tempted to overindulge at your next meal.

BYO BITES

If you're heading out for the day, pack a snack to take with you so you aren't tempted to grab a less-healthy option when hunger strikes. Pop some vegie sticks or fruit in a small container or keep a snack bar in your car. You'll save money, too!

PUT AWAY THE PACKET

When you are reaching into a bowl of popcorn or a big bag of chips, it's hard to know when to stop. A better plan is to transfer a portion into a small bowl or buy individual-sized packets so you can track the SmartPoints value more accurately.

TAKE YOUR TIME

Research has found that people who chew snacks slowly and more mindfully don't eat as much and feel fuller for longer. So challenge yourself to see how many times you can chew each mouthful (20 times is a good start). Chewing slowly rather than rushing your food also helps improve digestion.

HUNGER OR HABIT?

Do you automatically stop for morning tea at 11 am? It could be that your mind has been programmed to tell you it's time to eat, even if you're not hungry. To break the habit, try doing something else to refocus your mind – enjoy a brisk walk or clear out your emails.

LESS IS MORE

If you really want that decadent restaurant dessert, just say yes to a smaller portion. Ask for a thin slice or cut it in half to share with a friend. That way you don't miss out and you don't overdo it either.

DITCH DISTRACTIONS

Ever found yourself working at your desk and suddenly noticed your biscuit seems to have disappeared into thin air? Because you weren't concentrating your mind hasn't registered that you've already eaten it. Stop, enjoy your snack and then get back to what you were doing.

IN CLEAR SIGHT

Store healthy snacks where you can see them. Keep a well-stocked fruit bowl on the kitchen bench and have pre-cut vegie sticks in a clear container at eye height in your fridge so they are the first thing you see.

EAT REGULARLY

One of the biggest causes of overeating is undereating. That's because if you're starving by the time your meal hits the table you are more likely to want (and eat) more. So if you genuinely feel hungry and your next meal is at least an hour away, a well-timed snack can actually aid your weight loss.

WW Member story: *Pinki Vyas*

A NEW START

When Pinki Vyas' husband Sudheer got an engineering job in Australia in 2012, she was more than happy to relocate from India with her young children. But while she expected a quieter life without the congestion that came with living in New Delhi, Pinki says she noticed something unexpected. 'I grew up in a small town in India and for women, the priority is the house and family,' she says. 'When I came here, I saw the other school mums do drop-off in their active-wear, ready to go and do a fitness class. I loved how people looked after themselves here. It wasn't selfish – they just had an awareness of knowing what they needed to do for themselves.'

HITTING A PLATEAU

When Pinki decided to lose weight, she did what she thought she had to do: cut out meals and hit the gym religiously. 'I was starving and not eating enough, which was causing low blood pressure, dizziness and constant headaches,' she recalls. She managed to lose 7 kg on her own but hit a plateau and was miserable living such a restricted life. When her friend Rinky, a WW member, suggested she come to a WW Workshop, Pinki was reluctant, doubting the program would cater for her as a vegetarian. 'She pushed me, saying, "You don't know what it's about unless you go!"' Pinki recalls. 'She was right. You quickly learn exactly what you need to do.'

HEALTHIER TRADITIONAL FOOD

Much to Pinki's surprise, the first thing her WW Coach Ian got her to do was increase her portion sizes and stop skipping meals. 'I started eating at regular intervals with the right amount of protein and carbs. I now have three meals a day and two snacks and I feel so much better.'

Pinki learned clever ways to adapt traditional Indian foods so the whole family could still enjoy them and eat together. 'Instead of using cream and coconut milk in curries, I use 99 per cent fat-free yoghurt,' she says. 'If I need oil, I'll use spray or reduce the amount, such as using 4 teaspoons instead of 4 tablespoons. I'll add more vegetables as well.' Within three months she hit Goal and she's still there a few years later. 'It's been life changing for me,' Pinki says. 'I learned how to focus on the changes I wanted to make to my life.'

WALKING TO CONFIDENCE

Inspired by her new zest for life, Pinki's husband Sudheer started walking with her and before long had set his own goals. 'He was encouraged by the positive changes and started running and ended up competing in three marathons in a row!' Pinki enthuses. 'My son tracks the number of steps he takes on his fitness tracker and my daughter goes to the gym.' Being honest with herself, Pinki admitted she didn't enjoy the gym, so quit her membership to start walking in nature instead: 'I ended up doing 7 km every day.'

Through the process of living a healthier life, Pinki realised she was doing the very thing she had admired in women when she first arrived here 'I learned that if you take care of yourself first, everything else falls into place. My weight-loss journey gave me the self-confidence I needed.'

BECOMING A WW COACH

Pinki's extended family and friends were also in awe of her turn-around and were soon asking for pointers. 'I told them, "Start walking with me. It's free and it moves all of the muscles in your body."' Those walks gave Pinki an opportunity to share knowledge about the role of nutrition and healthy cooking in maintaining a healthy weight.

So great are her motivational skills that Pinki became an in-demand WW Coach in Sydney. 'WW started out as a good way to connect with people,' she says. 'It took time to develop fluency in English, as it's my second language, so I started as a second Coach, learning how the WW Coach put things together and helped people. I loved talking to people and helping them solve problems. My members and their achievements are my biggest source of inspiration and motivation.'

FIT, CONFIDENT AND IN CONTROL

In her quest for greater self-care, Pinki puts her hand up for just about any activity on offer. 'I wasn't a sporty person,' she says. 'Now I want to enjoy all sorts of different sports.' That meant skiing trips, running a 12 km fun run, doing Bollywood dancing and learning to swim. 'That was a really big thing for me,' Pinki admits. 'I thought I would sink in the pool. But I started walking in our pool and my daughter is teaching

Then

Now

'If you take care of yourself first, then everything else falls into place. My weight-loss journey gave me the self-confidence I needed.'

me to swim. It helps that I can wear bathers with confidence!'

Pinki says she never imagined that her life could be so different. 'A lot of my family are overweight and have chronic diseases, so it was hard-wired in my brain that I couldn't lose weight because it was in my genes. But once I hit Goal, I had an incredible sense of self-control – I realised that if I can control this, I can control anything!'

*Pinki lost weight on prior WW program and continued on *myWW*. Weight loss may vary.

Kitchen essentials

The simple act of organising your kitchen can have a huge impact on your health. This is because you're more likely to cook healthy food if you have the right set-up and ingredients on hand to do so.

Tips for an organised kitchen

Kitchens are a busy place. These tips will help you stay organised and make food prep a breeze.

1 CHECK YOUR PANTRY
Get rid of out-of-date items and stock up on new ingredients. Plan meals around items that are soon to expire.

2 USE SHELF ORGANISERS
Small containers and baskets (or even an unused shoe box!) will help you store smaller items neatly in easy-to-find locations.

3 TRY A LAZY SUSAN
For corner cupboards or pantries with deep shelves, try a spinning organiser to make maximum use of harder-to-reach areas.

4 LABEL, LABEL, LABEL
Label each shelf in the pantry (and fridge!) so everyone in the house knows where things go.

5 HAVE A PLAN
Make a meal plan for the week ahead so you know what you're cooking and when. Try to use soon-to-expire products first.

6 USE A WHITEBOARD
Attach a whiteboard or notepad to the inside of a cupboard door or fridge so you can instantly jot down things you need to buy.

Grow your own herbs

So many fresh herbs are thrown out because we only need a few leaves. Try growing your own herbs in a windowsill planter or a sunny spot in the garden, if you have space. You'll add some beautiful greenery to your home while reducing food waste.

Low-waste living

Not only is living sustainably better for the environment, it can be better for your wallet, too. Here are some tips to help minimise waste and leave a positive impact on the world around us.

1 BUY LESS, MORE FREQUENTLY
Replenish fresh produce and other perishables every few days, rather than buying a week's worth of groceries at once. Topping up your fresh produce more regularly means you're less likely to buy too much of something and end up throwing it away.

2 COOK ONLY WHAT YOU NEED
Unless you're intentionally doing a batch cook, measure ingredients accurately to ensure you cook only what you need. That way you're less likely to overcrowd your plate or throw away food at the end of the night.

3 PRESERVE SEASONAL PRODUCE
Preserve any leftover fruit and vegetables by turning them into low SmartPoints pickles, jams and chutneys.

4 STORE FOOD BETTER
Herbs and salad leaves wilt quickly if not stored properly. To make them last longer, wrap herbs in a damp paper towel and store in a sealed container. Store salad leaves, such as rocket or baby spinach, between dry paper towels inside an airtight container.

5 MAKE LEFTOVERS YOUR FRIEND
Uneaten leftovers make up a huge proportion of food waste. Use leftovers to make stocks and soups. Turn extra pasta or cooked vegies into frittatas or blend cooked vegies with canned tomatoes to create a vegie-packed pasta sauce.

6 FREEZE FOR LATER
Freeze par-cooked, pre-cut vegies to use for meals at a later date.

7 COMPOST
If you've got a garden or balcony, invest in a compost bin for your food scraps to turn your leftovers into natural, chemical-free, zero-cost fertiliser for your plants.

8 UNDERSTAND EXPIRATION DATES
'Baked on' dates are for baked goods, such as bread and pastries. They taste best on the day they're baked, but it doesn't mean they're inedible after that. 'Use by' means that you need to consume the product by that date. These dates are set by manufacturers as there may be safety concerns for foods after this date. The 'best before' date emphasises quality not safety. So if a food is past its 'best before' date, it may not be off, just not as fresh as it could be, such as chips or biscuits that have lost their crunch.

Inside *your* pantry

Set up your pantry in a way that better serves your health goals. Positioning healthy options at eye level means you're more likely to reach for them when you're hungry. The same goes for treats, so look to store them on the top shelf where they're out of sight and out of mind!

A well-organised pantry is not only lovely to look at, it can also make you a more efficient and healthier cook! It makes finding ingredients simple (so cooking is more enjoyable), cuts down on food waste (goodbye stale, half-used packets) and makes it easier to know when you need to stock up (no more ringing for takeaway because you forgot to replenish a vital ingredient).

Start by taking everything out of your pantry and discarding anything that's past its use-by date or looking (or smelling!) a bit dodgy. If you find perfectly good food that you just don't need (leftover Christmas treats, perhaps?), consider donating them to a neighbour or charity. Now, clean all the shelves (a vacuum is great for crumbs in crevices) and group similar items together (cans with cans, jars with jars, etc).

Middle shelf magic

The middle shelf is where most people's eyes will go first. For this reason, it's the best place to keep healthy foods. It's also a good place to stock the things you use regularly, such as tea, coffee and breakfast cereals. Arranging cereals here, where they're easy to see and reach, means children can help themselves to a healthy breakfast, too.

Your pantry

TOP SHELF
Best for treats, specialty items and alcohol

Keeping treats where they are harder to see (and reach) makes them less of a temptation. But if those chocolate biscuits are still calling your name, put them in a tub or opaque container.

Specialty items that you don't use very often, such as cake-decorating supplies and equipment, can be archived up here in dedicated containers.

The top shelf is also a good place for keeping cooking alcohol out of reach of children, and storing light bulky items, such as paper towels and party supplies.

SECOND SHELF
Best for dry goods (baking ingredients, grains, dried legumes, herbs, spices, etc)

Decant dry ingredients, such as pasta, rice, quinoa and dried legumes, into clear, similar-sized, airtight containers. This keeps out weevils and moisture, makes them easier to stack and helps you see if you are running low.

All the bits you need for baking come in a range of shapes and sizes, so store them together in stackable containers so they take up less room and are easy to locate.

Herbs and spices are best stored in the pantry as too much heat and light will affect the flavour. If you have a messy jumble of packets and jars, invest in a spice rack or container to keep them neat and tidy.

THIRD SHELF
Best for cans, bottles and Tetra packs (canned vegies, sauces, liquid stock, etc)

Stacking cans saves space but it can be hard to see them all. One solution is to buy (or make) tiers designed to elevate the back row. It also helps to separate your cans into sub-groups, such as legumes, tomatoes and fish.

Bottles have a habit of toppling over (and always seem to have a loose lid when they do!). Prevent this by storing oils, sauces and vinegars in baskets or pantry caddies lined with paper towel (to catch any drips).

Tetra packs of liquid stock, long-life milk and soup are easy to stack but tiered stands (like the one for cans) make life that little bit easier.

FOURTH SHELF
Best for snacks and breakfast needs (cereal, spreads, bread, tea and coffee, etc)

Place a selection of healthy snacks below your direct eyesight so you are not tempted every time you go to the pantry, but they are accessible when you need them. If you share your snacks with kids, pull-out baskets make it easy for them.

Want the kids to get their own breakfast? Then store the cereal at kid height! It is easier to tell when supplies are running low if you decant them into clear containers.

If everyone in your family wants a different spread on their toast, store the honey, peanut butter and Vegemite together in one basket that you can pull out of the pantry (and put back) with ease.

BOTTOM SHELF
(OR FLOOR)
Best for potatoes and onions, drink bottles, bulky or heavy items

To stop onions from sprouting and potatoes from turning green, they need to be stored, separately, in a cool, dark place in well-ventilated baskets. Don't store them together.

A large tub with wheels makes it easier to access heavy items at the back.

If you like to buy in bulk, store extra items in a plastic tub until you need them.

Inside *your* fridge *and* freezer

Believe it or not, there is a science to organising your fridge. Get it right and food will stay fresher for longer and will be much easier to find.

Your fridge

TOP SHELF
Best for cheese, butter/spread, milk, eggs, tofu and yoghurt

Keep these foods covered as they absorb odours easily. Eggs are best stored in the carton they are sold in.

Write the date you open tubs of yoghurt, sour cream or soft cheese on the lid and consume within the recommended period.

Hard cheese will keep for up to 3 months but if it develops surface mould, cut it off along with at least 2 cm of the cheese around it.

MIDDLE SHELF
Best for deli meat, cooked food and leftovers

Place cooled leftovers in the fridge within one hour of cooking (or bacteria will multiply). Divide large amounts of food into smaller portions so they cool more quickly.

Position leftovers at the front of the shelf in clear containers so you remember to eat them.

Store pre-sliced deli meat towards the back. Wrap in baking paper, then place in snap-lock bags and consume within 3 days. Packaged deli meat can be stored until the use-by date but follow the instructions once opened.

BOTTOM SHELF
Best for raw meat, chicken and seafood

Always store raw meats and seafood below food that will not be cooked to avoid possible cross contamination by food-poisoning bacteria. Place on trays to catch drips.

Store meat, poultry and seafood towards the back of the shelf (the coldest part) and consume within 2–3 days.

Defrost meat, chicken, seafood and leftovers in the fridge (allow at least 24 hours) rather than leaving them out on the kitchen bench.

CRISPER DRAWERS
Best for vegetables and fruit

Keep fruit and veg in separate crisper drawers if possible as fruit produces a gas (called ethylene) that can accelerate ripening. Avoid storing very ripe fruit with other fruit for the same reason.

To stop leafy greens and root vegetables becoming limp, store them in perforated (or loose) bags. Some crisper drawers have an adjustable vent to control air flow.

Only store stonefruit, mangoes, pineapples, pears, melons and avocados in the fridge once they have ripened. Place in perforated (or loose) bags and return to room temperature before eating.

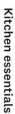

Check the temp

The ideal fridge temperature is below 5°C as this slows the growth of bacteria. Avoid overcrowding your fridge as it will have to work harder to maintain a safe temperature.

Top shelf

Middle shelf

Bottom shelf

Crisper drawers

In the fridge door

The temperature in the fridge door is always slightly warmer than other parts of the fridge, so store milk on the top inside shelf with other dairy goods if possible. Save the door shelf for low-kilojoule drinks and bottles and jars. Curry pastes, pesto and tomato paste will keep for longer if you cover the surface with a thin layer of olive oil. Alternatively, you can freeze them in ice-cube trays, then transfer to snap-lock bags and freeze for up to 2 months. Some bottles and jars don't need to be kept in the fridge until they are opened (such as jam and some Asian sauces). Others don't need to be kept there at all, such as honey (it will crystallise), coffee (it will lose its flavour), Vegemite, peanut butter and some sauces (the salt keeps them safe). Just check the package instructions to be sure and, if in doubt, put it in the fridge.

Don't forget to audit

Conduct regular fridge 'audits' to discard anything past its use-by date. A couple of times a year, take everything out and clean the shelves and crisper drawers with warm, soapy water.

Inside your freezer

The freezer isn't just for frozen peas and back-up loaves of bread, it's also your best friend when it comes to batch cooking. To keep your meals in the best possible shape, it's important to be across the basics of safe and effective freezing. Here is a list of top items for your freezer:

- ✳ Frozen fruit (e.g., berries and bananas)
- ✳ Frozen edamame, peas, spinach, broccoli and corn
- ✳ Chicken breasts
- ✳ Fish fillets and prawns
- ✳ Turkey and beef mince

Safe freezing times

FOOD	FREEZING TIMES
Cooked rice and rice dishes	1 month
Cooked meat	2–3 months
Soups	2–3 months
Meat- or chicken-based stews, curries and pasta sauces	2–3 months
Pasta bakes and cooked pasta	3 months
Cooked veg and legumes	3 months
Vegetable-based stews, curries and pasta sauces	4 months

TIPS FOR SAFE FREEZING

When done correctly, freezing food is an effective way to prevent bacteria from multiplying. If the temperature of the freezer is increased, not only can food be damaged, it can also allow bacteria to grow, compromising the safety of the food. Make sure that your freezer is not overfilled and the door is not kept open for longer than necessary so that the temperature is maintained.

Cool before freezing

To avoid increasing the temperature of the freezer, cool foods before placing them inside (but don't leave food out to cool for longer than 2 hours).

Freeze in small portions

Freezing meals in small portions not only helps food to cool down faster, which reduces the growth of bacteria, it's also a good way to portion meals and prevent waste.

Package it well

Place food in freezer bags (making sure to squeeze out any extra air) or sealed food-safe containers to protect it from freezer burn and contamination. If using containers for soups or other dishes with a high water content, remember to leave a little extra room for expansion.

Thaw safely

Food shouldn't be thawed at room temperature, as this can allow dangerous levels of bacteria to grow. To defrost your frozen foods safely, use the defrost setting on your microwave or place it on the bottom shelf of the fridge overnight. This last step is important, as keeping it on the bottom shelf prevents it from contaminating other foods if leakage occurs during defrosting.

WW Member story: *Sarah Van Dyke*

11 kg WEIGHT LOSS*

A WW TWIST ON TREATS

For anyone trying to lose weight, muffins are usually off the menu, but Sarah, a former home economics teacher, couldn't face a future without her favourite treat, so she set to work and devised a delicious muffin recipe with just 2 SmartPoints per serve.

Sarah has also put a WW twist on other delicious treats such as sticky date pudding, cream horns, apple pies, Eton mess, trifles, easy pasta bake and Tuscan chicken (just to name a few!). The recipe receiving all the accolades is her famous Nutella muffins. Each one has a spoonful of the chocolate–hazelnut spread in the centre and has only 2 SmartPoints.

GATHERING A FOODIE FOLLOWING

Sarah's recipes tick every box so it's not surprising that after she launched her Facebook page, Sarah's Recipes AUNZ, in December 2016, she had more than 7,000 fans within just 3 months. You can also follow her Instagram feed @sarahs_recipes.

Not only do people love her food, they love the results. 'They tell me, "Because of you, I can have my treats and still lose weight", but I just provide the recipes. They do the work.' Anyone still doubting that a person who eats muffins can lose weight and keep it off only has to look at Sarah's own success.

MANAGING EMOTIONAL EATING

Sarah initially joined WW in January 2011 after seeing a family photo of herself at Christmas. 'I thought, Gosh, you really need to do something about this,' she recalls.

She and her former husband and their daughter, Alyssa, had just returned from 16 months living in Chile, South America. 'I had really struggled there. Alyssa was only two, I missed my family, my husband was away working a lot and I did a lot of emotional eating. I used to lunch all the time with the other expat ladies. Everything seemed to revolve around food and alcohol, and eating healthily was expensive.'

At WW back in Australia, Sarah 'pulled up my big-girl panties' and tracked everything she ate. 'I still weigh and measure everything. It's the only way for me.'

BECOMING A WW COACH AND HELPING OTHERS

In 2012, Sarah was invited to be a WW Coach and leapt at the chance to help others feel as fantastic as she has done since her weight loss. She has now increased her involvement and works in other WW roles as a personal phone Coach. Her Facebook page is a labour of love – and probably the biggest job of all, as she responds to reader queries, devises recipes and taste-tests them on her lucky neighbours.

UPS AND DOWNS

The top of Sarah's Goal range is 71 kg. She previously crept up to 73 kg. 'I wasn't being kind to myself. I'd been through a divorce, I'd been helping Alyssa with her emotions, and I didn't give myself positive talk. There are times when life just becomes too difficult. I let myself go and went under. I'm now down to 70 kg and try to keep focused on changing my habits. People can achieve their Goal, but if they don't face their triggers they roll back into unhealthy habits.'

HELPING OTHERS LOSE WEIGHT AND ENJOY FOOD

There were tears when Sarah recounted her story at a WW event. 'I have 100 per cent care of Alyssa and I needed to do something for both of us,' she says. 'To be rewarded for that in front of my peers was massive.' Recently, Sarah was on the phone when a member asked for her name. Sarah recalls: 'She then asked, "Are you the Sarah from Sarah's Recipes? I'm about to make your banana muffins!" That's always happening and it's totally unexpected. I just wanted to help my group access my recipes and to use my home economics background to make sure even those who aren't confident cooks can follow them.'

MY RECIPE FOR SUCCESS

1 **Exercise** I love walking and live near the beach on the Sunshine Coast in Queensland. Walking on the sand enables me to work on my fitness and mindset. I switch off, immerse myself in the surroundings and give myself time to be me.
2 **Food** I eat fresh, in-season ingredients that are less expensive. Flavour is hugely important.

Then

Now

'At WW, we know how emotions influence weight loss.'

If a dish is boring, no-one wants to eat it. I always have good SmartPoints snacks on hand to stop me reaching for chips or chocolate. When planning meals, I start with protein and build around that.

3 **Mindset** It's important to focus on me, to be kind to myself and to know it's okay to have a bad week. I understand why and what to do about it. At WW, we know how emotions influence weight loss.

*Sarah lost weight on prior WW program and continued on *myWW*. Weight loss may vary.

Healthier cooking

At WW, we're all about making clever swaps, not cutting out all the foods you love. With a little planning and know-how, you can eat healthily without feeling like you're missing out.

* Choose lean cuts of meat and trim off all the visible fat.
* Remove the skin from poultry for an instant SmartPoints saving.
* Use non-stick pans for cooking (a quick spritz of oil spray or 1–2 teaspoons oil is usually enough to stop food from sticking). Try WW pan or oven liners. If cooking pieces of meat such as steaks, brush the meat with oil rather than the pan.
* Use olive, canola or sunflower oil for most cooking needs – they have the same SmartPoints as other oils but contain more antioxidants.
* Include flaxseed oil in dressings for extra omega-3 fatty acids.
* If stir-fried vegies are sticking to the wok, add a little water or reduced-salt stock instead of more oil. This will create steam to cook the vegies faster without burning them.
* Line baking trays and cake tins with baking paper. Again, this reduces the amount of oil needed for greasing.

* Try alternative natural sweeteners designed for baking (such as granulated stevia or xylitol) instead of sugar in cakes, muffins, slices and biscuits.
* Swap butter for reduced-fat spread in baking. In many cake and muffin recipes, you can also substitute half the spread for no-added-sugar apple puree or a mashed banana (this keeps the texture moist with less fat).
* Use a steamer or microwave to cook vegetables as they retain more nutrients.
* Choose reduced-salt and no-added-sugar products whenever you can.

Vegetables your way

When it comes to roasting vegies in particular, try using chicken, beef or vegetable stock as an alternative to oil. This will stop them from drying out and add a touch of flavour, while also keeping the SmartPoints value down. Drizzle a tablespoon or two of stock over vegies and toss to coat before roasting in the oven. Alternatively, you can braise vegetables by gently simmering them in a saucepan with stock until tender.

Make time to plan

Spending 15 minutes planning your meals will not only help you stay inspired and focused, but it will also minimise the challenge of thinking about what to have for lunch or dinner each day. Weekends are ideal for meal planning – with the extra time, you can prep, shop and cook in one go. If you have children, get them involved and prepare a recipe from this cookbook. Writing down your plan can help cement intention and keep you on track. Place your plan somewhere easily accessible. The fridge door is a good spot because it's at eye level and usually in a prominent position in the kitchen.

Cooking method tweaks

It's not just what you cook, but how you cook that can make a big difference to the SmartPoints value of any dish. One of the simplest ways to reduce fat and SmartPoints value is to minimise the amount of oil you use when making a meal. By using one of these smart tweaks, you can reduce your oil use by up to 100 per cent.

CLASSIC COOKING METHOD	SMARTER COOKING METHOD
Shallow-frying crumbed food or browning meat in ¼ cup oil	Lightly spray crumbed food with oil and pan-fry using a liner (silicone or baking paper). Eliminate oil altogether by using a lined tray in the oven, or use an air-fryer.
Deep-frying potato chips or wedges in oil	Lightly spray potato chips or wedges with oil and oven bake on a lined tray at 180°C for 30–40 minutes. Eliminate oil altogether by using an air-fryer.
Deep-fried battered fish in oil	Oven bake without batter, or grill using a dry rub seasoning and a light spray of oil.
Stir-frying meat or vegetables in batches using ¼ cup oil	Stir-fry using a non-stick wok and a light spray of oil.
Roasting meat with ¼ cup oil	Roast meat on a rack with just a light spray of oil.
Pan-frying fish or chicken in oil	Cook fish (10 minutes) or chicken (15 minutes) in a steamer lined with baking paper over simmering water without the need for oil.
Roasting vegetables around a whole chicken, leg of lamb, pork or beef roast with ¼ cup oil, plus absorbed fat from meat	Roast vegetables on a separate baking tray lined with baking paper with a light spray of oil.

Smart *swaps*

You can enjoy your favourite foods without compromising your nutrition goals. Switching a few ingredients in your go-to meals can have a big impact without sacrificing flavour. Here are some of our top swapping tips to help you build healthier meals.

BREAKFAST

* **Milk** is a breakfast staple and there are many different types to choose from. But whether your preference is for dairy, soy or nut-based milks, within each variety there are some healthier swaps you can make. Switching from full-cream milk to skim milk will significantly reduce the amount of kilojoules you're consuming. This is similar to the differences between regular soy milk and low-fat soy. In the case of nut milks, specifically seeking out unsweetened varieties will save you up to 10 g of added sugars per serve.

* **Fruit juice** is a regular breakfast addition; however, it can contain a lot of concentrated sugars (up to 4–5 teaspoons in a single glass). Choosing a vegetable juice will boost the overall nutrient content of your drink, lower the SmartPoints and cut sugar content.

* **Bread** options are varied, and the type of bread that you choose can make a massive difference to your overall nutritional intake. For example, large, thick slices of white bread can be very high in refined carbs, and Turkish and Lebanese bread can contain 3–4 times the amount of carbs of smaller traditional slices. Swapping to thin or even lower-carbohydrate varieties of bread that are whole grain-based can reduce the SmartPoints while boosting fibre.

* **Yoghurt** is another favourite at the breakfast table but did you know that some sweetened yoghurts can contain as much as 20 g (or 5 teaspoons) of added sugar per serve? Reduce your sugar intake by choosing plain, unsweetened or Greek-style yoghurts, which contain as little as 5–8 g of natural sugars per serve.

LUNCH

* **Salads** are a great choice, but many pre-made salad dressings are high in sugar and oil. For a lighter option, try adding extra virgin olive oil with a little balsamic vinegar for a serve of heart-healthy fats along with a boost of flavour.

* **Nutrient-rich spreads** such as avocado or hummus are great replacements for butter.

* **Wholemeal and whole grain varieties** are great choices when it comes to carbs. Where possible, choose whole grain bread, brown rice and whole grain crackers as healthier options. The extra fibre will help to control blood-glucose levels after eating and ensure that the digestive system has the nutrients it needs each day to function at its best.

* **Cheese** can be made healthier by opting for low-fat cottage cheese or ricotta. This smart swap will reduce the amount of saturated fat you're having.

DINNER

* **Stocks** go a long way in boosting the flavour of many meals, but they can also be packed full of salt, which can impact blood pressure. Seek out liquid stocks and stock cubes that contain no added salt, or that are salt-reduced.

* **Cooking oils** come in many varieties, but our top pick is antioxidant-packed extra virgin olive oil. Contrary to popular belief, olive oil can withstand high cooking temperatures while retaining its nutrient and antioxidant content, making it an ideal option for everyday cooking.

* **Baking paper** is a great way to reduce the SmartPoints of pan-based foods. We often reach for the butter or oil without thinking, but baking paper is an excellent substitute. Not only does this mean you do not need to add fat, it also helps to marinate the protein in any sauces.

* **Brown and whole grain varieties** should be your preference over refined carbs, such as rice and pasta. Choosing whole grains, such as quinoa, will add extra protein and fibre to any meal. Plus, boosting the fibre content of the meal will help you stay fuller for longer, and support gut health.

* **Vegetables** are an easy and healthy way to boost nutrition. Don't forget that you can easily substitute pasta with zucchini noodles and rice with cauliflower. Not only will you boost the fibre content of the dish, but you will also bump up your veg intake.

* **Sauces** can be lower in kilojoules, too! When you use bottled sauces, such as soy sauce, tomato sauce or mayonnaise, look for varieties that are labelled as 'no added sugar' or 'no added salt'.

SNACKS

* **Stevia-based baking blends** halve the use of added sugar, making this quick swap an easy way to lower the sugar content of any recipe. Another handy trick for healthy bakers is to use vanilla extract as a flavour enhancer to a range of recipes, including banana bread, mini muffins and protein balls.

* **Flour** is present in many recipes, but don't forget you can easily substitute a wholemeal flour. Higher-fibre snacks will help to keep you fuller for longer.

* **Frozen bananas** are a healthy option for those looking for something sweet. In fact, it tastes very similar to ice-cream, especially when blended, creating a lower-kilojoule alternative to your favourite ice-cream, custard or sweetened yoghurt.

Keep some simple swaps on standby

* Try spray oil instead of bottled oil to minimise the quantity you use.
* Swap noodles or pasta for spiralised vegie noodles or, alternatively, do half/half with your favourite pasta.
* Swap mashed potato for mashed cauliflower or parsnip.
* Enjoy chicken breast fillets where recipes call for chicken thighs.
* Try yoghurt instead of mayonnaise or cream in recipes.
* Thicken sauces with skim milk or cornflour instead of cream.
* Swap coconut milk for coconut-flavoured evaporated milk.

Vegetarian *and* vegan swaps

Transform your favourite dishes into delicious meals to suit your personal needs without compromising on taste. Use our simple ingredient swaps to make vegetarian or vegan eating a breeze.

Meat and seafood swaps

To make a dish vegetarian, simply swap out the meat or seafood for one of the following plant-based alternatives that are high in protein and iron:

TOFU

This vegetarian staple lends itself incredibly well to dishes such as stir-fries, noodles and curries. Tofu is made from soybeans which are a good source of protein and contain all nine essential amino acids.

TEMPEH

Made from fermented whole soybeans, tempeh offers similar nutritional benefits to tofu, but with a nuttier flavour and a meaty texture. Tempeh works well in stir-fries and curries, and is delicious when marinated and grilled to serve with vegetables, salad or in a burger.

SEITAN

Made from wheat gluten, the main protein in wheat, seitan is a popular meat alternative and can be used in similar ways to tofu and tempeh.

LEGUMES

Lentils, chickpeas and beans are a versatile, nutrient-dense alternative to meat. Lentils make great meat-free 'meatballs' and are an excellent beef alternative in bolognese sauce and chilli, while chickpeas and beans are delicious in stews, curries and even pasta.

Egg swaps

Eggs are often used as a binding ingredient in baking, but they can easily be replaced using one of the following:

* Mix 1 tablespoon ground linseeds/flaxseeds with 3 tablespoons water
* Mix 1 tablespoon chia seeds with 2½ tablespoons water
* ¼ cup aquafaba (brine from canned chickpeas)
* ¼ cup unsweetened apple puree
* ½ medium mashed banana.

Dairy swaps

Whether it's brunch or baking, there are lots of dairy-free swaps available. Where possible, choose products with added calcium and little or no added sugar.

MILK SWAPS

* Soy milk
* Almond milk
* Rice milk
* Light coconut milk.

CHEESE SWAPS

* Vegan cheese
* Nutritional yeast flakes
* Cashew cream cheese.

YOGHURT SWAPS

* Soy yoghurt
* Coconut yoghurt (note: made with coconut cream, so has a high saturated fat content)
* Silken tofu.

CREAM SWAPS

* Light coconut cream
* Cashew cream.

BUTTER SWAPS

* Dairy-free margarine
* Oil, such as extra virgin olive oil
* Avocado – spread on sandwiches or toast.

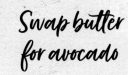

Swap butter for avocado

47

Equipment must-haves

To make cooking simple, it's worth investing in a few essential kitchen utensils. Use this list as a guide so cooking healthy dishes is a breeze!

BAKING PAPER

Reduce cooking oil by lining pans and trays with baking paper or try WW oven liners.

BOX GRATER

Not just for cheese, use this to turn cauliflower into cauliflower rice, grate citrus zest for a fresh finish on salads or fish, or use the large holes to grate hard-boiled eggs. Grate vegies, such as zucchini, directly into soup as it cooks for a last-minute vegie boost. Remember, grated vegies are very quick to cook, which can save you time in the kitchen.

COLOURED CUTTING BOARDS

Avoid cross-contamination of food by allocating specific coloured boards for different ingredients. For example, red for raw meat and chicken, green for fruit and veg, brown for cooked meat, blue for raw seafood and white for bread.

MEASURING CUPS AND SPOONS

Two must-have items for the most successful cooking results and for quicker, easier portions.

WW SILICONE LOAF TIN*

The shape of the mould includes imprints on the inside that allow you to perfectly portion the loaf into equal slices. This way you can cook for the whole family and enjoy a healthier portion of everything from banana bread and carrot cake, to savoury loaves and frozen desserts.

SILICONE SPOONS, SPATULAS, TONGS AND A WHISK

High-quality silicone utensils have more benefits than simply being bright and colourful. They won't scratch your pans and, when washed properly, won't harbour bacteria. Plus, they also won't crack, peel, melt or break down into the food as you're cooking.

NON-STICK POTS AND PANS

Essential for low-fat cooking, non-stick pots and pans require very little oil and make whipping up pancakes or stir-fries a breeze.

SHARP KNIVES

Including a 20 cm chef's knife and a serrated knife. Blunt or dull knives are dangerous because they need more pressure and are more likely to slip. If you don't know how to use a traditional knife sharpener, you can buy a hand-held one that helps remove the guesswork.

VEGETABLE PEELER

Peel apples, vegies and ginger or create thinly sliced vegie ribbons with this kitchen multi-tasker.

WW OMELETTE MAKER*

This will help you make delicious omelettes in the microwave in minutes. With a non-stick lining, it eliminates the need for oil, and it's dishwasher safe and BPA free. It also doubles as a handy steamer for your vegetables before you add them to your omelette.

SILICONE MITTS

High-grade silicone oven gloves are heat-resistant, even in very high temperatures – meaning there's less chance you'll get burned compared with cloth mitts. They're also easier to keep clean as they are non-porous and waterproof, so less likely to harbour germs.

STEAMER

The ultimate healthy cooking tool for a variety of ingredients, including vegetables, chicken and fish.

STICK BLENDER OR FOOD PROCESSOR

Use these kitchen essentials to quickly make your own sauces, smoothies and vegetable purees.

Other essential cooking tools

- ☐ Baking trays
- ☐ Kettle
- ☐ Microwave-safe and freezer-proof containers
- ☐ Mixing bowls
- ☐ Colander and sieve
- ☐ Wooden spoons
- ☐ WW non-stick pan liners*

*Find out more at ww.com/shop

WW Member story: *Jacqueline Nadis*

20 kg WEIGHT LOSS*

GROWING UP AS THE 'BIG KID'

If the difference between the possible and the impossible lies in a person's determination, then Jacqueline Nadis is that person. Looking at her today, it's hard to believe the 37-year-old mum of two has spent most of her life wishing she was invisible. 'I grew up being that 'big' kid,' says Jacqueline. 'I can't remember a time during my childhood when I didn't feel embarrassed about my body. I believed I was born to be big and there was nothing I could do about it. It was just who I was, but it was a terrible way to be. The stigma, the teasing. It scarred me.'

GAINING CONTROL

The turning point came in 2004 when Jacqueline was 21 and weighed 103 kg. 'Mum kept telling me I needed to lose weight. I was in a relationship at the time and I thought, I'm okay, I'm fine. Then a few months later when that relationship turned sour, I was a mess.' To help Jacqueline get over the break-up, her sister Angie booked a surprise trip to Italy. It was there that Jacqueline first proved to herself that she had control over her weight. 'I started to wonder why I was carrying all this weight. I felt like I was wasting my life,' she recalls. While on holiday, the girls walked for hours every day. When they returned home, Jacqueline found she had lost 9 kg in three weeks. 'I kept up my daily walking, but I knew I needed to do more,' she says. 'I had tried diets before,

but they had only made things worse. I was either constantly hungry and couldn't stick to the plan, or I would lose a few kilos only to pile them back on again once I stopped buying the special meals, which were also expensive.' It was then that a work colleague told Jacqueline about WW.

SMALL CHANGES, BIG RESULTS

Unlike the diets Jacqueline had been on in the past, she found WW offered a complete change. All her favourite foods were allowed, and tracking made her feel in control and accountable. 'Chips are my weakness,' she says. 'But instead of never letting myself even look at them, I would save up my Points and have them occasionally, so I never felt deprived.' In two years, Jacqueline lost 39 kg and reached her Goal. 'I felt so amazing. I'd spent all those years feeling self-conscious and sad. It was like I had been given my life back.'

HARD WORK PAYING OFF

Breaking old habits proved harder than she thought once Jacqueline stopped going to WW Workshops. Gradually, the weight crept up again. 'I had gained 7 kg since leaving home, but I knew WW worked, so I went back on the program and reached my Goal weight for a second time in just six months,' she said. 'It really is about having the right mindset. You can wake up every day and tell yourself you're going to eat healthily today, but if you're not in the right mindset it won't happen.'

FAMILY AND FREEDOM

In 2010, Jacqueline married Jonathan and their first child, Nicholas, was born in 2013. During her pregnancy, she gained 22 kg: 'I told myself it would all be fine after the birth. Of course, it wasn't.' When Nicholas was five months old, Jacqueline's weight had climbed to 87 kg.

Then Jacqueline spotted an email from WW offering half-price membership. It was the sign she needed. 'I had 23 kg to lose, but with Jonathan working and me being on maternity leave, I couldn't get to Workshops, so I did my third WW journey digital.' For Jacqueline, the WW digital program has been the best and most rewarding way to lose weight. 'I love the WW app! It's so flexible and I can do everything from home, which suits me and the boys. I missed Workshops at first because I liked meeting other people with similar goals, but now I connect with other members on the app. It's a great community that's always there for you during the highs and the lows. I got back down to Goal in eight months.' When their youngest son Sebastian was born, Jacqueline again gained weight, this time putting on 25 kg. 'I was 82 kg when I joined WW for the fourth time in August 2017, and lost 17 kg in 10 months,' she says. 'Because I was still breastfeeding, I was allowed more Points, so I could still have crumpets, which I craved.'

A few years later, Jacqueline is still kicking goals. Things she never thought possible are a reality, like ditching her high-blood pressure medications and taking up boxing. 'I have so much energy for my boys now and I know they are growing up loving their lives and feeling really good about themselves.'

Then & Now

MY TIPS FOR REACHING YOUR GOAL

1 **Believe in yourself** Nobody wants you to succeed as much as you do, so give it everything and do it your way.

2 **Never give up** Even when you have a bad day, just get back on track and keep going towards your Goal. It doesn't matter how long it takes, it only matters that you get there.

3 **Don't beat yourself up** We all make mistakes but giving yourself a hard time about it is a major motivation killer. Forgive yourself and move on. Every day is a new day.

4 **Listen to your body** Some days will be better than others and plateaus happen. That's when you need to train harder and get fierce!

*Jacqueline lost weight on prior WW program and continued on *myWW*. Weight loss may vary.

Meal planning

When it comes to healthy eating, meal planning is one of the most powerful things you can do. Not only does it help you keep on track with your food goals, but knowing what you are going to eat each week can save you time, money and reduce your overall food waste. To help get you started, here's our quick guide to mastering meal prep.

1 MAKE A PLAN

While meal planning may sound time consuming at first, it can actually be a very quick and simple process when you break it down. To begin with, set aside some time each week to decide which healthy meals and snacks you would like to prepare, take stock of what ingredients you already have, and make a list of what you will need to buy. Then, once you have your list, pick up the groceries (either in person or order online) and you are ready to go!

2 SET ASIDE TIME TO COOK

The second key to sucessful meal planning is to allocate time to get in the kitchen and start cooking. Despite the best of intentions, not planning can result in running out of time to cook, which can lead to wasting your ingredients. For this reason, planning, shopping and then cooking will work best if you do it on the same day when you have a couple of hours allocated to complete the process. As a general rule of thumb, one-pot meals such as bakes, soups and casseroles are among your best options. These meals are easy to make, freeze and store, and can be packed with plenty of delicious vegetables.

3 BREAK IT UP

Meal prepping doesn't just include cooking full meals all at once, it is also about streamlining healthy eating at every step of the process. This means doing as much of the food preparation as you can in advance so that it is easy to grab what you need throughout the week. This may translate into cutting up pieces of fruit or vegetables in advance; pre-making a couple of lunchtime salads; or whipping up some healthy patties or meatballs that you can cook quickly when you get home from work. For busy people on the go in the morning, breakfast can be tricky. Get your day off to a healthy start no matter how rushed you are by prepping your morning meals the night before. Breakfast muffins and overnight oats can be made in advance so all you need to do is grab and go as you walk out the door each morning.

4 DON'T FORGET SNACKS

While main meal prepping is important, don't forget about snacks, too! It's often when we are between meals and unprepared that we are likely to make less healthy food choices.
Set yourself up for success by whipping up some healthy homemade banana bread, mini muffins or protein balls in advance to keep on hand throughout the week. You can also pick up some of the specially designed WW snacks from your local Workshop or our website.

5 PACK YOUR FOOD THE NIGHT BEFORE

The final step to ensure that meal planning works in your home is to take a minute or two each night to get your food ready for the next day. This may mean packing yourself a lunchbox with leftovers, a healthy snack and cut-up vegetables. Or it may mean taking a frozen meal out of the freezer so that you have lunch or dinner ready for the next day. Again, allocating a small amount of time each day will go a long way to making sure that meal planning works for you.

Batch cooking

Batch cooking is a great way to ensure you've got healthy options on hand and don't fall into the takeaway trap. It involves preparing dishes in larger quantities and freezing the additional portions so that you have several meals ready to go. It doesn't need to be fancy or complicated. Essentially, you're cooking what you would normally cook – just more of it.

While batch cooking might require a little time up front, the time and freedom it returns to you later can be very rewarding. There are two main methods of batch cooking. The first is cooking up large quantities of a dish that can then be portioned and frozen to be enjoyed gradually across multiple meals. The second is preparing bulk amounts of a given ingredient, which can later be used in other dishes. For example, you could roast pumpkin and use it in soup on the following day or perhaps toss it into a salad or a frittata.

Foods that work best for batch cooking include:
* Curries, stews and soups
* Rice dishes
* Pasta sauces and bakes.

Components of meals can also be batch cooked:
* Rice, quinoa and pasta
* Vegetables and legumes
* Patties and meatballs.

Get clever with prep

When it comes to batch cooking, look at the ingredients you can easily prep in bulk. Items that come in handy might include a tray of mixed roasted vegies, poached chicken breasts or boiled eggs. Use them for quick lunches or dinners throughout the week or add them to stir-fries, stews, soups, grills, salads, curries, frittatas or pies. A food processor or stick blender with a mini-chopping attachment can be a great tool to help reduce the time spent prepping vegies, such as onions, celery and carrots. Buying in bulk can save money and any leftover vegies can be frozen. Alternatively, the freezer aisle in the supermarket is great for pre-prepared frozen vegetables.

Know how to scale your recipes

Batch cooking generally involves doubling, tripling or even quadrupling a recipe; however if you're cooking for one or two and don't plan on freezing extra serves, you may want to halve a recipe. Here are our tips for scaling recipes.

1 GET IT IN WRITING FIRST
Write down your adjusted ingredient quantities before you start cooking to help you stay on track.

2 EGGS CAN BE MESSY
If you end up needing only half an egg after halving a recipe, crack it into a bowl, whisk to combine the yolk and white and then measure out half.

3 NOT ALL FOODS ARE EQUAL
When scaling recipes, the same conversion factor can't be applied to all ingredients. If you're doubling a recipe:
* Increase seasoning by 1.5 rather than 2, then adjust to taste.
* When sautéing, you only need enough oil to cover the base of the pan.

4 COOKING TIMES CAN DIFFER
Cooking times may need to be adjusted when scaling recipes up or down. If scaling a recipe up, check the recipe at the time specified, then continue checking every few minutes until it's ready. If reducing the quantity, begin checking before the specified cooking time.

5 TEMPERATURES MAY VARY
As a general rule, if halving a recipe, reduce the oven temperature by 10°C and if doubling, increase by 10°C. The same rule applies for stovetop recipes; you will need to go up or down a little depending on the quantities.

What *is* a serve?

The following is a guide to healthy portions, and how much of each food group to eat each day to ensure you're getting the nutrients you need.

VEGETABLES

Each day aim for at least 5 serves of vegetables.

What's a serve?

* 1 small (or ½ medium) potato
* 1 cup raw salad/green vegetables
* ½ cup (85 g) cooked dried or canned beans or lentils.

FRUIT

Each day aim for 2 serves of fruit.

What's a serve?

* 2 small pieces of fruit (such as plums, apricots, mandarins or kiwifruit)
* 1 medium-sized piece of fruit (such as an apple, banana, orange or pear)
* 1 small bunch of grapes
* 1 cup chopped fresh fruit salad
* 1 cup canned fruit (with no added sugar).

PROTEIN

Each day aim for 2–3 serves of lean protein.

What's a serve?

* 65 g cooked lean beef, lamb, veal or pork (90–100 g raw)
* 80 g cooked lean poultry (100 g raw)
* 100 g cooked fish fillet (115 g raw)
* 2 large eggs
* 170 g tofu
* 30 g nuts, seeds or peanut/almond butter
* 1 cup cooked legumes (such as lentils, chickpeas or cannellini beans).

DAIRY OR ALTERNATIVES

Each day aim for 2.5 serves of low-fat dairy or fortified alternatives (3 for teenagers or breastfeeding mums and 4 for women over 50).

What's a serve?

* 1 cup (250 ml) low-fat dairy or soy milk
* ½ cup (125 ml) low-fat evaporated milk
* 200 g 99% fat-free plain or no-added-sugar flavoured yoghurt
* 2 slices (40 g) reduced-fat hard cheese
* ½ cup (100 g) low-fat or reduced-fat ricotta or cottage cheese.

CEREALS & GRAINS

Each day aim for 3-6 serves of cereals/grains (preferably whole grains).

What's a serve?

* 1 slice (40 g) wholemeal or whole grain bread
* ½ medium (40 g) wholemeal or whole grain bread roll
* ½ cup (75–120 g) cooked rice, pasta, noodles, barley, quinoa or polenta
* ½ cup (120 g) cooked porridge
* ⅔ cup (30 g) wheat cereal flakes
* 2 (30 g) wheat-flake or oat-flake breakfast biscuits
* ¼ cup (30 g) natural (untoasted) muesli.

HEALTHY FATS

Each day try to incorporate healthy fats. You can get these from oils such as olive, canola, sunflower, sesame or flaxseed/linseed oil. Nuts, seeds and avocados also contain healthy fats – a small handful of nuts or ¼ of an avocado should fulfil your daily needs.

DRINK UP

Drink 6–8 non-alcoholic drinks a day (water is ideal). Aim for no more than 2 standard alcoholic drinks a day and include a few alcohol-free days each week.

Protein
2 large eggs

Fruit
1 small bunch
of grapes

Protein
80 g cooked
lean poultry

Cereals &
grains
½ cup
(75–120 g) cooked
rice or pasta

Dairy
2 slices (40 g)
reduced-fat
hard cheese

Dairy
200 g 99% fat-free
plain yoghurt

Healthy
fats
small handful
of nuts

Fruit
2 small pieces

Healthy
fats
¼ avocado

Protein
65 g cooked
lean beef

3 steps *to a* healthier plate

It's important to learn how to balance your plates (don't worry, there is no crockery juggling involved!).

A balanced plate (or meal) contains the three main food groups we need to stay healthy:

* vegetables (non-starchy)
* lean proteins (meat, poultry, fish, tofu, eggs, dairy, legumes, etc)
* carbohydrates (includes whole grains and starchy veg).

It should also contain a small amount of healthy fats, which are essential for many body functions. Many of us have grown up eating meals where protein and carbohydrates take up most of the plate. However, for better balance you should try and serve meals that are more like the plate opposite.

Use this as a guide for most of your meals and it will make a huge difference – not just for weight loss but your overall health. Sticking to sensible portion sizes is important for weight-loss success. Here are some tips on how to serve up a healthy plate.

1 USE SMALLER PLATES
Research shows that eating from a larger plate means you're likely to serve and eat more food.

2 GO FOR CONTRAST
People serve themselves 30 per cent more food when the plate and the food are the same colour (for example: white rice on a white plate).

3 BUY SINGLE-SERVE PACKS
A great idea for foods such as chips and ice-cream.

4 DIVIDE AND CONQUER
If you buy food in bulk, check the nutritional information to work out how many serving sizes are inside. Divide the contents into individual serves so it's easier to keep track of what you're eating.

5 EAT MINDFULLY
Eat without distractions, such as TV. Cut your food into bite-size pieces, chew slowly and place your cutlery down between mouthfuls. This will give your body time to signal to the brain that it's full.

Use your hand

Here are some helpful ways to judge your portions when eating out:

* **Palm** = 1 serving of meat, poultry or fish
* **Fist** = 1 cup (for example: one serving of fresh fruit, salad or green leafy vegetables)
* **Fingertip** = 1 teaspoon (for example: one portion of light cream cheese, chilli sauce or tartare sauce)
* **Thumb tip** = 1 tablespoon (for example: one portion of reduced-fat Italian dressing, ricotta or low-fat cheese)
* **Cupped palm** = ½ cup (for example: one serving of rice, lentils or pasta)

½ plate
Non-starchy
vegetables

¼ plate
Whole grains or starchy
vegetables

¼ plate
Protein

Eating out

Eating out? Use these tips to help you make healthier choices!

1 USE ZEROPOINT FOODS TO PLAN AHEAD

If you want to order your favourite pasta or dessert, try to eat lower SmartPoints options earlier in the day.

2 BEFORE YOU GO, LOOK UP THE MENU ONLINE

Check the SmartPoints value of dishes using your WW app or WW Shop and Eat Out guide, so you have a plan before you arrive. Try to order first so you won't be swayed by what others choose to order.

3 USE YOUR WEEKLY SMARTPOINTS AND ROLLOVERS

These SmartPoints give you more flexibility throughout the week. Leading up to your outing, plan how many SmartPoints you want to have available and save or roll over what you think you might need during the week. This will help you to stay on track to achieve your wellness goals.

4 ASK FOR DRESSINGS AND SAUCES TO BE ON THE SIDE

That way you can determine exactly how much you would like to add.

5 UNDERSTAND THE LINGO

'Smothered', 'rich', 'au gratin' and 'creamy' usually indicate higher SmartPoints values. 'Grilled', 'poached', 'steamed' and 'baked' tend to be lower in SmartPoints.

6 DON'T BE SHY ABOUT SPECIAL REQUESTS

Ask to swap chips for a salad with your main course or vegetables with balsamic vinegar instead of butter. (Unless, of course, you want them – in which case, track and enjoy!)

7 IT'S OKAY TO LEAVE FOOD ON YOUR PLATE

It's common in some cultures to leave food on the plate, signalling compliments to the host that they've been more than generous with the meal. So, stop when you're satisfied, instead of when you're overly full, and ask for a container for leftovers.

8 BE MINDFUL OF PORTION SIZES

If you enjoy having both an entrée and a main, you may want to consider choosing from the entrée options for both meals.

9 BE SALAD SAVVY

Creamy dressings, croutons, bacon, avocado, nuts and seeds are flavoursome but are also higher in SmartPoints. Ask for these on the side so you can add the amount you want.

10 ENJOY YOURSELF

If you want it, and it's worth it to you, track it and enjoy every bite! If you go over, it's fine. Make a plan the next day to get back on track.

Top tips
for takeaway

Although takeaway foods can be enjoyed as part of a healthy-eating plan, many servings can be larger than usual, plus the dishes can be high in sodium and kilojoules. Here's our guide on how to make smarter choices.

CAFE BRUNCH

* Swap fried or scrambled eggs, which can be cooked with generous amounts of butter or oil, for poached eggs.
* If you want to enjoy a plate of pancakes, look for ones made with healthier whole grains like buckwheat flour, and swap the whipped cream topping for yoghurt and fresh fruit.
* Breakfasts can be large when eating out – consider sharing one with a friend and ask for a fruit salad on the side to bulk up your meal.

CHINESE

* Swap battered or deep-fried dishes for steamed or sautéed.
* Choose dishes with plenty of vegies, such as steamed broccoli or stir-fries.
* Many Chinese dishes are made to order, so don't be shy about asking if your meal can be cooked with less oil.

ITALIAN

* Choose lean protein options, such as grilled calamari, fish or chicken dishes.
* For pasta, swap creamier sauces for fresh tomato-based ones.
* For pizza, opt for prawns or vegetables as your toppings instead of processed meats.

INDIAN

* 'Tandoori style' means the dish has been oven-grilled and is healthier than deep-fried foods.
* When choosing curries, opt for a dhal or vegetable curry instead of a creamy butter chicken.
* Go for roti over naan bread. It's made with wholemeal instead of white flour.

JAPANESE

* A warming umami-rich miso soup is a great low SmartPoints way to start your meal.
* If you're getting a salad, ask for the dressing to be put on the side.

* There are many fish options on Japanese menus, including sashimi. If you're not partial to raw fish, look for grilled fish or lean meat and skip the tempura.

THAI

* Swap creamy soups that use coconut milk for broth-based soups instead.
* Chicken skewers and rice paper rolls are healthier choices. Ask for the sauce on the side.
* Choose dishes that are sautéed with aromatic herbs, such as basil or lemongrass, and be mindful of dishes that are cooked in sauces, which can be higher in sugar.

PUB

* Ask if you can have your fish grilled instead of fried.
* Substitute your chips or fries with steamed vegies or salad.
* Try a spirit mixed with soda and lime or a low-alcohol beer for lower SmartPoints options.

WW Member story: *Mandi Adams*

DREAMING OF BIKINI CONFIDENCE

Mandi Adams will never forget her 'a-ha' moment. 'I was at the beach with my husband Ricky. Under my dress I was wearing the first bikini I had owned since I was 14, but I just couldn't find the courage to show it off.' Mandi said to Ricky, 'Look at that girl. She has cellulite like me but she looks fabulous in her bikini.' He said, 'Yes, and so do you.' Then she saw another woman. 'Look, she has stretchmarks like mine but how good does she look in that two-piece?' Again Ricky replied, 'Yes, and so do you.'

'I used to feel so ashamed about how I looked,' Mandi says. 'Ever since I was a teenager I've been consumed with self criticism. But, as we sat there, I realised that what I'd been seeing as physical flaws were really just part of who and what I am – a wife and mother in my 30s who is learning to be kind to herself' Moments later she tore off her dress and sprinted into the sea.

HIDING THE TRUTH

Mandi's weight problems began when she turned 18. 'That's when I started drinking and partying. Life was all about being a social butterfly and the weight crept up. 'I was the life of the party – but really, it was a show to cover up how embarrassed I felt about being overweight. I was ashamed about the way I looked, and I let that consume me.'

Now 35, Mandi and her husband Ricky, 40, have two children, Xavier and Sunny. 'I put on weight during both my pregnancies and had even joined WW and lost 10 kg after Xavier was born, but I put it all back on again when I had Sunny. 'I stopped going to WW Workshops and my eating got out of control again. I started binge eating as soon as the kids went to bed and sometimes I'd go to bed feeling so sick and upset with myself.'

SHIFTING HER MINDSET

At 29, Mandi was diagnosed with intracranial hypertension – a condition caused by too much pressure on the brain and spinal cord. 'I'd get the worst headaches and my eyesight suffered. An eye specialist and a neurologist both suggested I lose weight. Being overweight isn't linked to intracranial hypertension, but they agreed it would help if I was a healthy weight.'

With Mandi's illness mostly under control, the couple wanted to plan a holiday. 'But I didn't want to go on holiday overweight and miserable. I didn't want my kids to see me complaining about how uncomfortable I was.' Mandi joined WW for a second time. 'I went back because I knew it worked. With WW I'm always in control. I can spend my SmartPoints on anything I like as long as I track it all. It's when I stop tracking that I can get into trouble.'

Healthier foods, fresh meals at home and managing portion sizes all helped, but mostly Mandi knew she needed to shift her mindset. 'I believe healthy eating is a form of self-care and self respect. When I eat well, I feel better about everything else in my life. I used to say, "I just need to lose weight" but it's become much more than that. Now I say, "I'm choosing to do the things that make me feel good about myself." I love the flexibility of WW. Less weighing and less tracking means more time to enjoy my meals.'

GETTING STRONGER

Mandi stopped focusing on what she didn't like in the mirror and started noticing herself looking healthier and stronger. 'I've chosen a mindset that helps me eat well and exercise, because it nourishes my whole being, not just my body.'

Finding bootcamp after losing her first 10 kg, Mandi found she had energy to burn. 'The first time I thought I was actually going to die, but gradually it got easier. I used to hold weekly bootcamp sessions at home with a few girlfriends. The trainer would come to us. We did everything – weights, sprints, burpees and squats. It was so much fun and I always felt amazing afterwards. I still workout every day for a minimum of 30 minutes at home for my physical and mental health. I mix it up between body weight HIIT sessions, walks and runs,' she says.

THE TIME OF HER LIFE

Mandi's hard work has paid off in more ways than one. Not only does she feel proud of herself when she looks at photos from the family holiday, she's now medication free. 'I stopped taking medication for intracranial hypertension. I'm having the best time of my life and I feel it will be for the rest of my life.'

Then

Now

'Healthy eating is a form of self-care and self respect. When I eat well, I feel better about everything else in my life.'

3 THINGS I LOVE ABOUT WW

1 It is easy to fit into my everyday life, and it's about healthy eating for life.
2 Less weighing and less tracking of ZeroPoint foods leaves me more time and Points for foods I wouldn't normally track.
3 Eggs, salmon and chicken are my favourites and they're ZeroPoint foods on the Blue and Purple food plan. Awesome!

*Mandi lost weight on prior WW program and continued on *myWW*. Weight loss may vary.

WW day *on* a plate

Green

Looking for some guidance on what to eat when following the Green plan? We've got you covered. These filling and healthy options are sure to keep you satisfied all day.

Morning tea

Keep some snacks handy for when hunger hits. A piece of fruit or a small handful of nuts are options you can easily reach for at any time.

Breakfast

Start your day with something filling and delicious like **Eggs Benedict** (page 100). If you're looking for something quick to grab and go, try a **Breakfast bar** (page 90) or low-fat Greek yoghurt with fresh fruit.

Lunch

For a quick, protein-packed lunch make a simple salad using microwave rice, fresh salad mix, a small can of 4 bean mix and a can of tuna. Otherwise try the **Hearty steak sandwiches** (page 168) or for a lighter lunch option why not try the **Vietnamese chicken salad** (page 160).

Afternoon tea

Vegie sticks with **Pumpkin hummus** (page 128) or a slice of **Banana loaf** (page 110) are more substantial snacks that will keep hunger at bay in-between meals.

Dinner

A simple oven-roasted salmon fillet with salad is a great dinner option if you're looking for something light. If you like to have a glass of wine with dinner, keep the SmartPoints of your main down to ensure you have room in your Budget for this. For a low SmartPoints option, try the **Zoodle bolognese** (page 236) or the **Creamy chicken and mushroom hot pot** (page 210).

WW Member and Coach Michelle Goff shares her top tips for following the Green food plan:

✴ Use your SmartPoints wisely to get more bang for your buck, but don't be afraid to use a lot of Points in one meal because you always have ZeroPoint fruit and vegetables to lean on to bulk up other meals.

✴ Even though on Green you have fewer ZeroPoint foods to choose from, you can still enjoy them exclusively as a meal or a snack. Hello, fruit salad and pumpkin falafels!

✴ Planning is key. We tend to plan main meals, but snack planning is even more important.

✴ WW food products are a lifesaver; I know at a glance how many SmartPoints are in the snack and there's no guesswork.

✴ Spend time organising your pantry and fridge. If good food is readily available, you'll be more likely to reach for it instead of the chocolate bickies.

WW day *on* a plate

Blue

For meal inspiration on the Blue plan, why not enjoy these delicious dishes that are sure to give you the energy you need to get through a busy day.

Morning tea

If you like a morning cup of coffee or tea, you can enjoy it with an **Apple crumble muffin** (page 114).

Breakfast

Prep overnight oats the night before for a no-fuss breakfast option you can grab and go in the morning. Try **Zucchini, corn and haloumi fritters** (page 104) for some delicious new flavour combos.

Lunch

You can't go past the **Greek-style lamb wraps** (page 174) for a great low SmartPoints option that's easy to prepare.

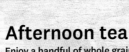

Dinner

Want something super quick and easy? Why not try the **BBQ chicken pizza** (page 240) or make a simple ZeroPoint stir-fry with sliced chicken breast and your favourite vegies.

Afternoon tea

Enjoy a handful of whole grain crackers paired with a simple **Tzatziki dip** (page 128)

WW Ambassador and Member Victoria Somers gives her top tips for following the Blue food plan:

* Bulk up every recipe with extra veg to make it more filling.
* If you really want your chocolate, wine or cheese fix, allow for it by tracking it early in the day so you don't blow the Budget by dinner time.
* For fussy eaters: hide green veg when you can. I peel zucchini and grate it to add to meals. None of my kids has a clue!
* Meal plan with the same ingredients. For example, we buy one large wombok and make two consecutive meals with it.
* Trust the program and the science behind it!

Purple

WW day
on a plate

The Purple plan is all about embracing ZeroPoint foods. Make the most of them with these tasty recipes that are packed with nutritious ingredients.

Lunch

Looking for something easy to pack for the work day? The **Sweet potato and chickpea patties** (page 148) are the perfect midday meal that can be prepared and packed ahead of time.

Breakfast

For a nutritious and hearty breakfast, warm up a bowl of oats with low-fat milk and a drizzle of honey. For something on the go, try Anna's 90-second mug muffin (page 84).

Afternoon tea

Make a super quick
**Crispbread topped with
beetroot dip and chicken**
(page 130), or grab some fresh
fruit salad and 99% fat-free
plain yoghurt.

Dessert

Is there still room for
dessert? ALWAYS! Finish
the day with **Banana and
passionfruit ice-cream**
(page 276).

Dinner

Enjoy a delicious **Easy pasta
bake** (page 182) or grilled
chicken breast with roasted
potatoes and salad for a
ZeroPoint dinner.

WW Ambassador and Coach Wendy Van Staden shares how she stays on track with the Purple food plan:

* I love *myWW* as nothing is off limits as long as you track. Tracking is the most vital tool and our WW app is so user-friendly for this.

* Use the barcode scanner in the WW app – I would be lost without that tool!

* I enjoy socialising and I enjoy a glass of wine or two. It is important to me that I keep my journey real and liveable.

* I absolutely love pasta, especially lasagne, so I love that the lasagne wholemeal sheets are ZeroPoints on Purple. I find that I am fuller for longer and snack less.

* Most importantly is that I have found it's easier on Purple to prepare meals the whole family can enjoy because we all love rice, potatoes and pasta. I have also enjoyed moving the family onto whole grain rice and pasta.

Sweet *and* creamy

Looking to give your meal a boost? Try these delicious additions for a sweet or creamy hit.

Apple sauce
2 teaspoons

Honey
2 teaspoons

Chocolate sauce
1 teaspoon

Maple syrup
1 teaspoon

Sweet

Cranberry sauce
1 teaspoon

Dried currants
2 teaspoons

Dried apricot
1 teaspoon

Mango chutney
2 teaspoons

Baba ganoush
1 tablespoon

Hummus
1 tablespoon

Mashed avocado
1 tablespoon

Low-fat ricotta
2 tablespoons

Creamy

Reduced-fat cream
1 tablespoon

Sun-dried tomato pesto
1 tablespoon

Basil pesto
1 tablespoon

Low-fat mayonnaise
1 tablespoon

Horseradish cream
1 teaspoon

Salty *and* crunchy

Add texture and flavour to your dishes with these tasty salty and crunchy elements.

Miso paste
1 tablespoon

Olives
2 tablespoons/
6 olives

Salty

Short-cut bacon
3 slices,
trimmed and
pan-fried

Canned anchovies
8 fillets

Parmesan cheese
¼ cup

Pepitas (pumpkin seeds)

2 teaspoons

Roasted peanuts

2 teaspoons

Crunchy

Roasted chickpeas

20 g

Pita bread

¼ toasted

Flaked almonds

1 tablespoon

Dressings *and* sauces

When it comes to flavour, a little can go a long way. Use these ingredients in the quantities listed to give any meal a boost.

Fat-free dressing
2 teaspoons

Dressings

Balsamic vinegar
2 teaspoons

Harissa
2 teaspoons

Mustard
3 teaspoons
(Dijon or wholegrain)

The WW Essential Guide to Healthy Eating

Soy sauce
1 tablespoon

Sauces

**Sweet chilli
sauce**
1 tablespoon

Tomato sauce
1 tablespoon

**Sriracha
(hot chilli
sauce)**
2 teaspoons

**Sesame
oil**
2 teaspoons

WW Member story: *Melinda Woollen*

33 kg WEIGHT LOSS*

ALL THE FAD DIETS

For 20 years, on and off, Melinda had been trying to lose weight. 'I tried all the shakes and meal replacements, everything,' she recalls. 'The weight would start to come off and then I'd think I could do it on my own, and I'd put it all back on.'

Melinda split from her husband when their kids were four and six, and she became a very busy single mum: 'I did all the day-to-day things on my own: dropping them off at school and all the sporting commitments, right through to teaching them how to drive. I worked full-time as well, which didn't leave a lot of time for looking after myself.'

Night-time became Melinda's downfall. 'Once they were in bed and the chores were done, I'd snack in front of the TV. Twisties were my weakness.'

In 2014, when Melinda was 48, she went on holiday to Hawaii with some girlfriends. 'I'd lost a few kilos before the break but until I saw the photos I hadn't fully realised how big I was,' she recalls.

Melinda's mother had died of cancer at the age of 49 and Melinda didn't want her kids to go through the same trauma. 'I was only 24 when Mum died,' she says. 'My kids were almost the same age – 20 and 22 – so I just thought, I've got to do something.'

CELEBRATE THE LITTLE WINS

Melinda's friend Morag was following WW and inspired by her success, Melinda joined WW, too. At first she fell into a self comparison trap. 'I'd hear other people say they'd lost a kilo or two and I'd think, I've only lost 300 g.' Her Coach Marie kept her motivated and reminded her that a loss is a loss – and it all adds up.

Inspired by her success, Melinda's sister also joined WW. Then her daughter joined, too. 'We've had quite a few friends and friends-of-friends who've joined, so there's a group of about nine of us that all catch up over coffee after the WW Workshops.'

Melinda says Workshops have become one of the highlights of her week. 'To get together with people who understand what you're going through and to celebrate the little victories – it is really empowering.'

DISCOVERING A LOVE OF FITNESS

At first, Melinda chose walking as a way to exercise and after six months of WW she built up the confidence to join a gym. 'I never used to be able to run and jump around, but now I do Aquafit and Dance Fit classes and Pump. I've also bought a bike. I love having the time for myself and I can feel myself getting fitter.'

Before, catch-ups with friends were always food-oriented. 'We'd go out for lunch or tea but we've swapped that for a walk or a ride. We might have coffee afterwards but we're a lot more active. And because there's a group of us doing WW together, it's always easy to find someone to go on a walk with.'

NO MORE ACHES AND PAINS

Before joining WW, Melinda – as a full-time administration manager– would have entire days when she wouldn't move from sitting at her desk. 'I knew I needed to add more movement into my life so I bought a stand-up desk and walked around the block a couple of times during my lunch break.'

When Melinda was overweight, her knee gave her a lot of pain. 'I got to the point where I thought I'd have to have surgery. I don't have any issues at all now so it was obviously weight-related.'

FINDING HEALTHY SUBSTITUTES

Prior to starting WW, Melinda didn't think about the foods she was eating. 'Breakfast was normally muesli, but after I began WW I saw it was quite high in sugar. Now I have overnight oats with berries and skim milk or a pancake.' Her favourite banana pancake is mashed banana, one egg and 1 tablespoon of self-raising flour. 'I serve it with berries and a drizzle of no-sugar maple syrup.'

FAMILY PRIDE

Melinda used to stay home because she couldn't find anything she felt looked nice but now she loves going out. 'My kids are pretty proud, too!' she says. 'When I got to Goal, my daughter Amber announced it on Facebook and said, "So proud of my mum", so that was really nice to see.'

Then

Now

MY TIPS FOR GETTING THROUGH A TOUGH WEEK

1 **Have a visual** I had little progress jars with beads for every 100 g I wanted to lose. After my WW Workshop, I'd transfer them from one jar to another.

2 **Look at the big picture** Keep looking back to where you've come from. If you have a little gain, look at how much you've lost overall.

3 **Use your support system** Don't think, 'I've had a bad week, I'll skip my WW Workshop.' You'll get back on track faster if you get support.

4 **Ask for help** I used to say to my son, 'If you haven't seen me going to the gym for a few days, say something.' It really helped.

*Melinda lost weight on prior WW program and continued on *myWW*. Weight loss may vary.

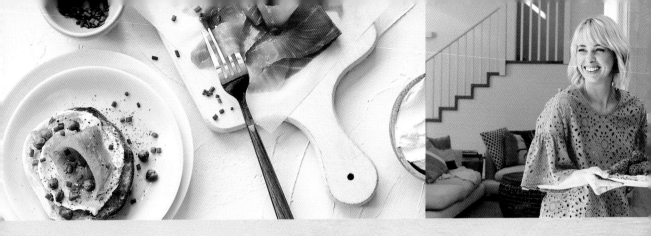

PART TWO

The recipes

Breakfast

3-ingredient banana pancakes

 SmartPoints value per serve

PREP 10 MIN / **COOK** 5 MIN / **SERVES** 1

1 small ripe banana

1 egg

2 tablespoons wholemeal
   self-raising flour

1   Mash banana in a bowl until smooth. Whisk in egg, then flour until smooth. Set aside for 5 minutes.

2   Lightly spray a non-stick frying pan with oil and heat over medium heat. Spoon 2 tablespoons batter into the pan and spread out with the back of a spoon until 1 cm thick. Repeat with remaining batter to make two more pancakes.

3   Cook for 1–2 minutes or until golden underneath. Turn over and cook for 1–2 minutes or until pancakes are cooked through. Serve.

Cook's tip

Serve with extra sliced banana, plus cinnamon butter (contains dairy) made with 2 teaspoons reduced-fat oil spread mixed with a pinch of cinnamon. Check your WW app for the SmartPoints.

The WW Essential Guide to Healthy Eating

Anna's 90-second mug muffin breakfast

5 **3** **0** SmartPoints value per serve

PREP 5 MIN / **COOK** 2 MIN / **SERVES** 1

⅓ cup (30 g) quick oats

1 ripe banana, mashed

pinch of ground cinnamon

1 egg

2 medjool dates, pitted
   and chopped

¼ cup (30 g) sliced strawberries

1   Place oats, banana, cinnamon, egg and dates in a
    410 ml microwave-safe mug and stir to combine.

2   Clean inside rim of mug with paper towel. Microwave,
    uncovered, on High (100%) for 90 seconds or until top
    is just firm. Serve with strawberries.

Cook's tip

Serve with 99% fat-free plain yoghurt
(contains dairy). Check your WW app
for the SmartPoints.

Member recipe
by Anna Van Dyken.
See more of Anna's
recipes @feedmehealthy_
annavandyken

Breakfast slice

3 **1** **0** **SmartPoints value per serve**

PREP 15 MIN / **COOK** 1 HOUR / **SERVES** 6

¼ cup (50 g) brown rice

100 g baby spinach leaves

6 eggs

1 carrot, coarsely grated

1 zucchini, coarsely grated

⅓ cup (80 g) 97% fat-free
   cottage cheese

120 g cherry tomatoes, halved

mint leaves, to serve

1   Place rice and ½ cup (125 ml) water in a small saucepan over high heat. Bring to the boil. Reduce heat and simmer, covered, for 25 minutes or until rice is just tender.

2   Preheat oven to 180°C. Line a 26 cm x 16 cm (base measurement) rectangular slice tin with baking paper, allowing paper to hang over the two long sides.

3   Place spinach in a large bowl. Add enough boiling water to cover. Stand for 30 seconds or until just wilted. Drain well.

4   Whisk eggs in a large bowl until combined. Season with salt and pepper. Stir in cooked rice, spinach, carrot and zucchini. Pour into prepared tin and distribute evenly. Dollop cottage cheese over the top. Use the back of a spoon to lightly press cheese into egg mixture. Bake for 30–35 minutes or until golden and set.

5   Cut into slices and serve topped with the cherry tomato and mint leaves.

Cook's tip

Store slice in an airtight container in
the fridge for up to 4 days.

The WW Essential Guide to Healthy Eating

Shakshuka

 SmartPoints value per serve

PREP 15 MIN / **COOK** 35 MIN / **SERVES** 4

1 red capsicum, chopped

1 yellow capsicum, chopped

1 eggplant, chopped

400 g can diced tomatoes

1 tablespoon herb and garlic
   pizza sauce

2 teaspoons ground cumin

½ teaspoon sweet paprika

1 teaspoon chilli flakes

4 eggs

½ cup coriander sprigs

⅓ cup (80 g) 99% fat-free
   plain yoghurt, to serve

1   Lightly spray a non-stick frying pan with oil and heat
    over medium–high heat. Add capsicums, eggplant and
    2 tablespoons water and cook, stirring, for 10 minutes
    or until softened. Add tomatoes, pizza sauce, cumin,
    paprika, chilli flakes and ½ cup (125 ml) water and bring
    to the boil. Reduce heat and simmer for 15–20 minutes
    or until vegetables are very tender and sauce is thick.

2   Using the back of a large spoon, make four hollows in
    sauce. Carefully, break an egg into each hollow. Cover and
    simmer for 5–6 minutes or until eggs are cooked to your
    liking. Sprinkle with coriander and serve with yoghurt.

Cook's tips

* Serve with sliced high-fibre
  whole grain bread (35 g slice per
  serve) (contains gluten). Check
  your WW app for the SmartPoints.

* Suitable to freeze (without eggs
  or toppings) for up to 3 months.
  Alternatively, store sauce in an
  airtight container in the fridge
  for up to 3 days.

Breakfast bars

4 **4** **3** SmartPoints value per serve

PREP 10 MIN / COOK 25 MIN / SERVES 24

80 g reduced-fat oil spread

⅓ cup (120 g) honey

2½ cups (225 g) rolled oats

½ cup (75 g) pepitas
(pumpkin seeds)

½ cup (75 g) dried apricots,
chopped

½ cup (75 g) dried cranberries

1 cup (250 ml) no-added-sugar
apple puree

1 egg, lightly beaten

1 teaspoon ground cinnamon

½ teaspoon mixed spice

¼ teaspoon salt

1 Preheat oven to 160°C. Lightly spray a 30 cm x 20 cm lamington tin with oil. Line base and sides with baking paper.

2 Place spread and honey in a saucepan over medium heat. Cook, stirring, for 1 minute or until melted and combined. Remove from heat. Add remaining ingredients and stir until well combined.

3 Spoon mixture into prepared tin and spread evenly over base. Bake for 25 minutes or until golden and firm. Transfer to a wire rack to cool. Once cooled, remove from tin and cut into 24 pieces. Serve.

Cook's tips

* Serve with fruit such as strawberries, banana or melon.

* Bars will keep in an airtight container for up to 4 days.

Breakfast tortilla

7 **7** **6** SmartPoints value per serve

PREP 5 MIN / **COOK** 5 MIN / **SERVES** 2

1 cup (270 g) baked beans
   in tomato sauce

1 tablespoon lime juice

2 x 36 g gluten-free tortillas

⅓ cup (80 g) 97% fat-free
   cottage cheese

1 tomato, chopped

30 g baby spinach leaves

1   Place baked beans in a small saucepan over medium heat. Cook, stirring, until hot. Stir in lime juice.

2   Heat tortillas following packet instructions. Top half of each tortilla with bean mixture. Spoon over cottage cheese and top with tomato and spinach. Roll to enclose filling. Serve.

Cook's tip

You can add ½ teaspoon chilli powder when cooking the beans if you'd like a little heat.

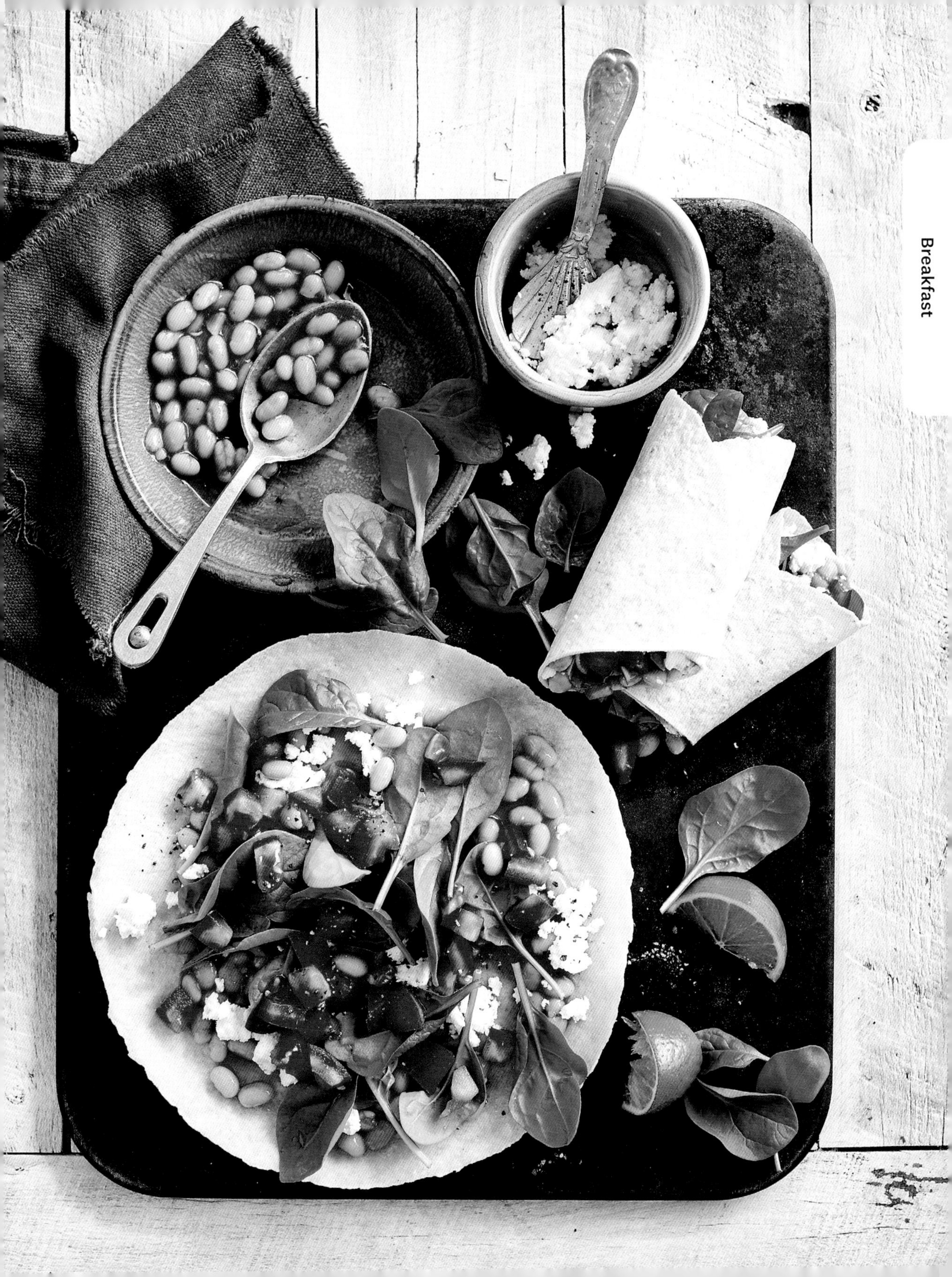

Breakfast hash
with poached eggs

5 **3** **2** **SmartPoints value per serve**

PREP 10 MIN / **COOK** 35 MIN / **SERVES** 4

250 g baby potatoes, halved

135 g short-cut bacon, fat
 trimmed, coarsely chopped

1 red onion, sliced

200 g mushrooms, sliced

200 g cherry tomatoes, halved

2 teaspoons wholegrain mustard

1 tablespoon chopped
 flat-leaf parsley

4 eggs

1 Place potato in a large saucepan, cover with cold water
   and bring to the boil. Simmer for 15 minutes, then drain
   well and set aside.

2 Lightly spray a large non-stick frying pan with oil and
   heat over medium–high heat. Cook bacon for 5 minutes.
   Remove and set aside.

3 Lightly spray pan again, cook onion and potato, stirring,
   for 5 minutes. Add mushroom and tomato and cook,
   stirring, for another 5 minutes. Season and stir in
   mustard, half the parsley and cooked bacon.

4 Meanwhile, half-fill a large deep frying pan with water and
   bring to a simmer. Carefully crack one egg into a cup, then
   slide egg into water. Repeat with remaining eggs. Poach
   eggs gently for 3–4 minutes or until egg whites are set
   and yolks are still soft or cooked to your liking.

5 Divide hash among four plates and top with a poached
   egg. Season to taste and sprinkle with remaining parsley.

Cook's tip

Add 2 cups baby spinach leaves
with mushroom and tomato in
step 3.

The WW Essential Guide to Healthy Eating

Maple-roasted bacon *and* poached egg muffins

 5 4 4 SmartPoints value per serve

PREP 10 MIN / **COOK** 15 MIN / **SERVES** 6

1½ tablespoons maple syrup

1 teaspoon ground cumin

6 x 40 g slices short-cut bacon,
    fat trimmed

6 eggs

3 wholemeal English muffins,
    split open

1   Combine maple syrup and cumin in a small bowl. Lightly spray a large non-stick frying pan with oil and heat over medium heat. Add bacon and cook, brushing with maple mixture, for 4–5 minutes or until crisp. Drain on paper towel.

2   Half-fill a large deep frying pan with water and bring to a simmer. Carefully crack one egg into a cup, then slide egg into water. Repeat with two more eggs. Poach eggs gently for 3–4 minutes or until egg whites are set and yolks are still soft or cooked to your liking. Using a slotted spoon, transfer to a heatproof plate. Cover and place in oven to keep warm. Repeat with remaining eggs.

3   Meanwhile, grill or toast muffins. Serve muffin halves topped with bacon and eggs and seasoned with pepper.

Serve with baby rocket leaves.

The WW Essential Guide to Healthy Eating

Smoked salmon *and* cream cheese muffin

 SmartPoints value per serve

PREP 5 MIN / **SERVES** 1

½ English muffin, toasted

2 teaspoons light cream cheese

1 x 25 g slice smoked salmon

1 teaspoon baby capers,
   rinsed and drained

1 teaspoon chopped chives

1   Spread muffin with cream cheese. Top with salmon.
    Serve sprinkled with capers and chives.

Serve with lemon wedges,
if desired.

Eggs benedict

 8 **3** **3** SmartPoints value per serve

PREP 5 MIN / **COOK** 15 MIN / **SERVES** 1

1 egg yolk

1 teaspoon lemon juice

¼ cup (60 g) 99% fat-free
plain yoghurt

1 teaspoon Dijon mustard

2 x 25 g slices short-cut bacon

2 eggs

1 x 35 g slice whole grain bread,
toasted

chopped chives, to serve

1. Combine egg yolk, lemon juice and yoghurt in a heatproof bowl. Place bowl over a saucepan of water, ensuring base of bowl is not touching water. Bring water to a gentle simmer. Cook, whisking, for 5–8 minutes or until thickened. Whisk in mustard until combined.

2. Meanwhile, heat a small non-stick frying pan over medium–high heat. Cook bacon for 2 minutes each side until crisp.

3. Place Egg Poacher Insert into Omelette Maker. Crack one egg into each cup. Close and microwave on Medium (70%) for 50–60 seconds, or longer for firm poached eggs. Carefully spoon out eggs.

4. Top toast with bacon, eggs, hollandaise and chives. Season with salt and pepper and serve.

Cook's tips

* Serve with baby spinach leaves.
* This recipe uses the WW 2 in 1 Egg Poacher and Omelette Maker. You can purchase this from the WW Shop (ww.com/shop).

The WW Essential Guide to Healthy Eating

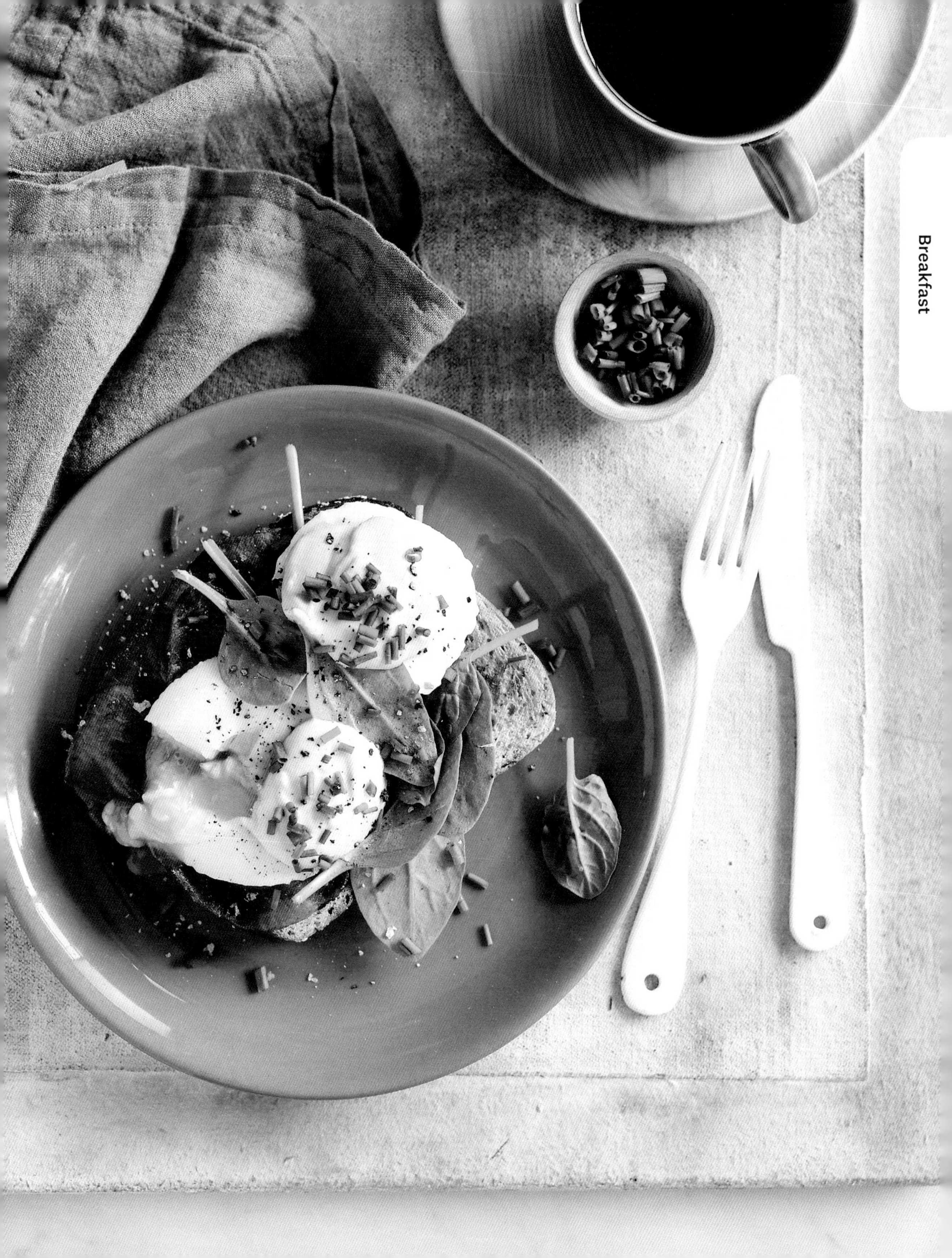

Spanish brunch

 SmartPoints value per serve

PREP 10 MIN / **COOK** 15 MIN / **SERVES** 4

250 g potatoes, cut into
   2 cm cubes

1 red onion, coarsely chopped

2 red capsicums, cut into
   2 cm cubes

120 g chorizo sausage, sliced

1 garlic clove, crushed

100 g button mushrooms,
   quartered

4 tomatoes, cut into wedges

2 teaspoons paprika

4 eggs

1 tablespoon flat-leaf
   parsley leaves

1   Cook potato in a saucepan of boiling water for 10 minutes or until just tender. Drain.

2   Meanwhile, spray a large non-stick frying pan with oil and heat over medium heat. Cook onion and capsicum, stirring, for 2–3 minutes or until softened. Add chorizo and cook, stirring, for 2 minutes or until chorizo is browned. Add garlic and mushroom and cook, stirring, for 2 minutes or until tender. Add tomato and paprika and cook, stirring, for 5 minutes or until tomato has softened. Add potato and stir to combine.

3   Place Egg Poacher Insert into Omelette Maker. Crack one egg into each cup. Close and microwave on Medium (70%) for 50–60 seconds, or longer for firm poached eggs. Carefully spoon out eggs. Repeat with remaining two eggs.

4   Serve potato mixture topped with poached eggs and parsley leaves.

Cook's tips

* This recipe uses the WW 2 in 1 Egg Poacher & Omelette Maker. You can purchase this from the WW Shop (ww.com/shop).
* Sebago potatoes are ideal for boiling. For a touch of heat, add 1 long red chilli (finely chopped) with onion in step 2.
* Swap chorizo for 400 g can black beans (drained and rinsed), if preferred.

Zucchini, corn *and* haloumi fritters

 SmartPoints value per serve

PREP 15 MIN / **COOK** 15 MIN / **SERVES** 4

1 small zucchini, grated

⅔ cup (100 g) self-raising flour

1 teaspoon sumac (see tip)

½ cup (125 ml) skim milk

1 egg, separated

½ cup (80 g) canned corn
   kernels, drained and rinsed

100 g haloumi cheese, grated

2 green shallots (spring onions),
   thinly sliced, plus extra,
   julienned, to serve

⅓ cup (80 g) 99% fat-free plain
   Greek yoghurt

lemon wedges, to serve

1   Combine zucchini and ½ teaspoon salt in a colander set
    over a bowl. Set aside for 10 minutes to drain.

2   Meanwhile, sift flour and sumac into a bowl. Place milk
    and egg yolk in a small jug and mix until well combined.
    Make a well in the centre of flour mixture and pour in
    egg mixture. Whisk batter until smooth.

3   Using electric beaters, beat egg white in a clean, dry bowl
    until soft peaks form. Gently fold egg white into batter.
    Squeeze excess moisture from zucchini. Add to batter
    with corn, haloumi and sliced shallot and fold gently until
    combined.

4   Lightly spray a large non-stick frying pan with oil and heat
    over medium heat. Spoon heaped tablespoons of batter
    into pan and spread out with a spoon to 1 cm thick. Cook
    for 2–3 minutes each side or until browned and cooked
    through. Transfer to a plate. Cover to keep warm. Repeat
    with remaining batter to make 12 fritters. Serve with
    yoghurt, julienned shallot and lemon wedges.

Cook's tips

* Serve with salad made with
   1 chopped Lebanese cucumber,
   2 chopped tomatoes, ½ thinly sliced
   red onion and 400 g can chickpeas
   (drained and rinsed). Check your
   WW app for the SmartPoints.

* Sumac is a purple-red spice with a
   lemony flavour. It is available in the
   spice aisle of supermarkets.

The WW Essential Guide to Healthy Eating

Snacks

Healthy zucchini slice

 SmartPoints value per serve

4 2 2

PREP 10 MIN / **COOK** 50 MIN / **SERVES** 6

1 leek, white part only, washed
    and thinly sliced
750 g zucchini, thinly sliced
8 eggs
½ cup (40 g) finely grated
    parmesan
¼ cup (35 g) plain flour

1   Preheat oven to 160°C. Line base and sides of a 20 cm (base measurement) square cake tin with baking paper.

2   Lightly spray a large non-stick frying pan with oil and heat over medium heat. Add leek and 1 tablespoon water and cook, stirring, for 5 minutes or until soft (add a little more water to help soften if needed). Stir in zucchini. Cook, covered, for 5 minutes, stirring once, or until zucchini softens but holds its shape. Set aside to cool.

3   Whisk eggs, parmesan and flour in a large bowl until combined. Season with salt and pepper. Add cooled zucchini mixture and stir to combine. Pour mixture into prepared tin and smooth surface. Bake for 40 minutes or until centre is just set. Stand in tin for 10 minutes. Use baking paper to lift slice from tin. Cut evenly into 6 pieces and serve.

Cook's tips

* For extra flavour, add ⅓ cup chopped flat-leaf parsley or basil with cooled zucchini mixture in step 3.

* Serve with salad of rocket and cherry tomatoes, drizzled with balsamic vinegar.

Sarah's banana loaf

 SmartPoints value per serve

PREP 10 MIN / **COOK** 35 MIN / **SERVES** 12

6 medjool dates, pitted
   and chopped
200 g rolled oats
5 ripe bananas
3 eggs
2 teaspoons vanilla extract
2 teaspoons baking powder
1½ teaspoons ground cinnamon

1   Preheat oven to 180°C. Lightly spray a 10 cm x 20 cm loaf tin with oil and line with baking paper.

2   Combine dates and 1 tablespoon boiling water in a microwave-safe bowl. Cover and microwave on High (100%) for 1 minute. Mash dates with a fork.

3   Process oats, 4 bananas, eggs, vanilla, baking powder, cinnamon and date mixture in a food processor until smooth.

4   Spoon mixture into prepared tin and smooth surface with back of a spoon. Slice remaining banana in half lengthways and arrange over top of loaf. Bake for 35 minutes or until a skewer inserted into the centre comes out clean.

5   Set loaf aside in tin for 5 minutes before transferring to a wire rack to cool. Cut into 12 slices and serve.

Member recipe
by Sarah Van Dyke.
See more of Sarah's recipes
@sarahs_recipes

Anna's apple pie bliss balls

2 **2** **1** SmartPoints value per serve

PREP 15 MIN + CHILLING / **SERVES** 15

100 g rolled oats

12 medjool dates, pitted

1 tablespoon maple syrup

2 tablespoons no-added-sugar apple puree

½ cup (40 g) desiccated coconut

½ teaspoon vanilla extract

½ teaspoon ground nutmeg

1 teaspoon ground cinnamon

1   Process oats, dates, maple syrup, apple puree, ⅓ cup (25 g) coconut, vanilla, spices and a pinch of salt in a food processor until a thick paste forms.

2   Place remaining coconut in a small bowl. Using wet hands, roll a tablespoon of mixture into a ball and roll in coconut to coat. Shake off excess and repeat to make 15 balls. Cover and chill in fridge until firm.

Cook's tip

Apple pie bliss balls will keep in a container in the fridge for up to 2 weeks.

Anna's cocoa bliss balls

2 **2** **2** SmartPoints value per serve

PREP 15 MIN + CHILLING / **SERVES** 20

100 g raw almonds

2 tablespoons cocoa powder

10 medjool dates, pitted

2 teaspoons honey

1 tablespoon maple syrup

¼ cup (20 g) desiccated coconut

1   Process almonds, cocoa, dates, honey and maple syrup in a food processor until a thick paste forms.

2   Place coconut in a small bowl. Using wet hands, roll 3 teaspoonfuls of almond mixture into a ball and roll in coconut to coat. Shake off excess and repeat to make 20 balls. Cover and chill in fridge until firm.

Cook's tip

To make chocolate-orange balls, add the zest of 1 orange and a good squeeze of juice into the mixture.

Member recipe
by Anna Van Dyken.
See more of Anna's recipes
@feedmehealthy_annavandyken

Sarah's apple crumble muffins

3 **2** **2** SmartPoints value per serve

PREP 10 MIN / **COOK** 20 MIN + COOLING / **SERVES** 6

6 medjool dates, pitted
  and chopped
½ teaspoon bicarbonate of soda
385 g can apple slices
  (see tip page 262)
¾ cup (115 g) self-raising flour
1½ teaspoons ground cinnamon
2 eggs, lightly beaten
2 teaspoons brown sugar
2 teaspoons reduced-fat
  oil spread

1   Preheat oven to 180°C. Line a 6-hole (¾-cup capacity) Texas muffin tin with paper cases.

2   Combine dates and ¼ cup (60 ml) boiling water in a large microwave-safe bowl. Microwave, covered, on High (100%) for 1 minute. Add bicarbonate of soda and mash dates with a fork (mixture will foam).

3   Process half the apple in a food processor or blender until smooth. Reserve 2 tablespoons flour. Add remaining flour, pureed apple, 1 teaspoon cinnamon and egg to date mixture and stir until just combined.

4   Combine reserved flour, sugar and remaining cinnamon in a bowl. Using fingertips, rub in spread until mixture resembles coarse breadcrumbs.

5   Spoon 1 tablespoon date mixture into each paper case. Top each with one-sixth of the remaining apple slices. Spoon the remaining date mixture over apple to cover. Sprinkle crumble mixture evenly over the top.

6   Bake for 18–20 minutes or until golden and a skewer inserted into the centres comes out clean. Stand muffins in tin for 5 minutes before transferring to a wire rack to cool.

Cook's tip

Store muffins in an airtight container for up to 2 days, or freeze for up to 2 months.

Member recipe
by Sarah Van Dyke
Find more of Sarah's recipes
@sarahs_recipes

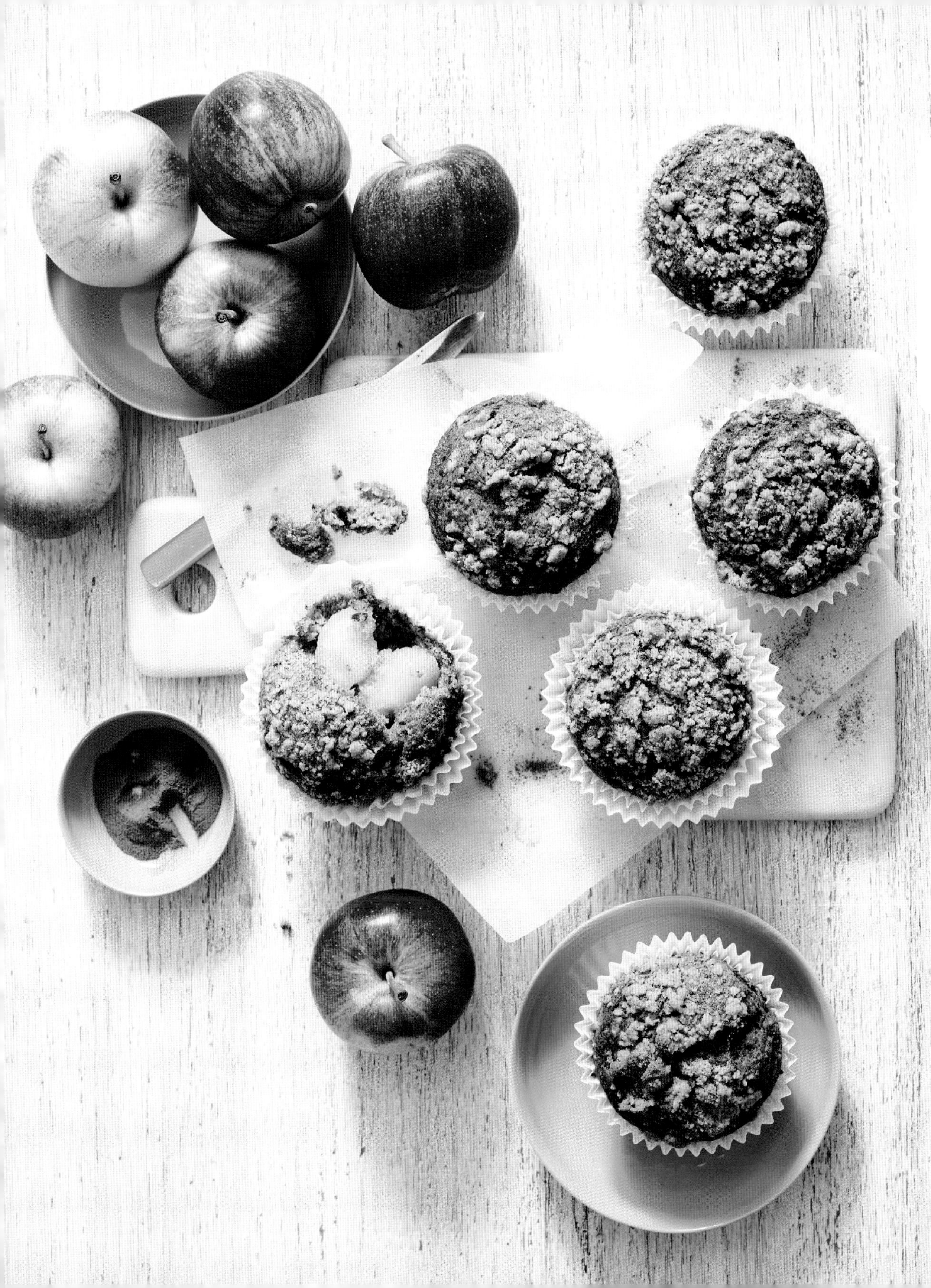

Sarah's chocolate Nutella-filled muffins

(2) (2) (2) SmartPoints value per serve

PREP 15 MIN / **COOK** 20 MIN / **SERVES** 15

8 medjool dates, pitted
   and chopped
½ teaspoon bicarbonate of soda
2 eggs, lightly beaten
1 ripe banana, mashed
½ cup (75 g) self-raising flour
1 teaspoon cocoa powder
85 g Nutella

1 Preheat oven to 180°C. Line 15 holes of two 12-hole (30 ml capacity) mini muffin tins with paper cases.

2 Place dates in a large microwave-safe bowl and add 1½ tablespoons boiling water. Stand for 1–2 minutes. Microwave dates on High (100%) for 1 minute. Add bicarbonate of soda and mash dates (mixture will foam up). Whisk in eggs and banana until combined. Sift flour and cocoa over egg mixture. Stir until well combined.

3 Spoon 2 teaspoons of batter into each paper case. Add 1 teaspoon Nutella to each. Cover with remaining batter. Bake for 15 minutes or until golden and tops spring back when lightly touched.

Cook's tips

* Use a very ripe banana for maximum sweetness and flavour.
* Mini muffin tins are available from specialty kitchen shops and most major supermarkets. Use a 24-hole tin if you don't have two 12-hole tins.

Member recipe
by Sarah Van Dyke
Find more of Sarah's recipes
@sarahs_recipes

Sarah's date muffins

 SmartPoints value per serve

PREP 10 MIN / **COOK** 20 MIN + COOLING / **SERVES** 8

16 medjool dates, pitted
   and chopped
1 teaspoon bicarbonate of soda
¼ cup (35 g) self-raising flour
2 eggs, lightly beaten

1   Preheat oven to 180°C. Line 8 holes of a 12-hole (⅓-cup capacity) muffin tin with paper cases.

2   Combine dates and ⅓ cup (80 ml) boiling water in a large microwave-safe bowl. Cover and microwave on High (100%) for 1½ minutes. Add bicarbonate of soda and mash dates with a fork (mixture will foam).

3   Add flour and eggs to date mixture and stir until just combined. Spoon evenly into paper cases. Bake for 15 minutes or until deep golden and a skewer inserted into the centres comes out clean. Stand muffins in tin for 5 minutes before transferring to a wire rack to cool. Serve.

Cook's tip

Store in an airtight container for up to 2 days, or freeze for up to 2 months.

Member recipe
by Sarah Van Dyke
Find more of Sarah's recipes
@sarahs_recipes

Snack boxes

Use recipes from the following pages to build your own snack boxes for those days when you're on the go. Here are some ideas for filling and delicious snack box combos!

The WW Essential Guide to Healthy Eating

	YOUR FAVOURITE DIP	DIP IT	SAVOURY SNACK	ADD SOME SWEETNESS
Snack box 1	Spinach and dill dip (page 126)	WW Sweet chilli lime nibblies	Mini Thai chicken patties (page 122)	Anna's cocoa bliss balls (page 112)
Snack box 2	Pumpkin yoghurt hummus (page 128)	Celery sticks and cherry tomatoes	Spice-roasted vegetable and cottage cheese frittata (page 124)	Mixed berries
Snack box 3	Roasted beetroot dip (page 126)	WW Cheese and onion chips	Easy sausage rolls (page 140)	99% fat-free yoghurt with lemon zest and blueberries
Snack box 4	Tzatziki (page 128)	Carrot and cucumber sticks	Pumpkin falafels (page 122)	Chopped fruit salad

Pumpkin falafels

 SmartPoints value per serve

PREP 20 MIN + CHILLING
COOK 40 MIN / **SERVES** 4

1 red onion, finely chopped
2 x 400 g cans chickpeas,
    drained and rinsed
750 g roasted pumpkin
3 garlic cloves, crushed
1½ teaspoons ground
    cumin
1½ teaspoons ground
    coriander

1 long red chilli, finely
    chopped
2 tablespoons chopped
    coriander
2 tablespoons chopped
    flat-leaf parsley
150 g 99% fat-free
    plain yoghurt
2 teaspoons lemon juice

1   Preheat oven to 220°C. Lightly spray a non-stick saucepan with oil and heat over medium heat. Cook onion, stirring, for 8–10 minutes or until softened. Remove from heat and set aside.

2   Process chickpeas in a food processor until a chunky puree forms.

3   Mash pumpkin in a large bowl. Add onion, chickpeas, two thirds of the garlic, cumin, coriander, chilli and chopped herbs. Stir until well combined. Shape mixture into 12 balls and place on a baking tray lined with baking paper. Chill for 20 minutes.

4   Bake falafels for 20–30 minutes or until golden. To make dressing, combine yoghurt, lemon juice and remaining garlic in a small bowl. Serve falafels with yoghurt dressing.

Mini Thai chicken patties

 SmartPoints value per serve

PREP 15 MIN / **COOK** 15 MIN / **SERVES** 20

500 g chicken
    breast mince
2 green shallots
    (spring onions),
    finely chopped
¼ cup finely chopped
    coriander

1 teaspoon lemon zest
2 tablespoons lime juice
2 tablespoons sweet
    chilli sauce
3 teaspoons fish sauce
2 teaspoons brown sugar

1   Place mince, shallot, coriander and lemon zest in a large bowl. Season with salt and pepper and mix until combined. Roll heaped tablespoons of mixture into balls and flatten slightly to form 20 small patties.

2   To make dipping sauce, combine lime juice, sweet chilli sauce, fish sauce and brown sugar in a small bowl. Stir until sugar has dissolved. Set aside.

3   Lightly spray a large non-stick frying pan with oil and heat over medium heat. Cook patties, in batches, for 3 minutes each side or until cooked through. Serve with dipping sauce.

Cook's tip

Swap chicken breast mince for turkey breast mince, if preferred. SmartPoints stay the same.

Spice-roasted vegetable *and* cottage cheese frittata

 SmartPoints value per serve

PREP 10 MIN / **COOK** 25 MIN / **SERVES** 4

8 eggs

¾ cup (180 g) 97% fat-free
cottage cheese

2 tablespoons chopped
flat-leaf parsley

3 green shallots (spring onions),
thinly sliced

2½ cups (375 g) mixed roasted
vegetables

1 teaspoon harissa paste

1 Preheat oven to 200°C. Line a 3 cm deep, 16 cm x 26 cm
(base measurement) baking tin with baking paper.

2 Whisk eggs and cottage cheese in a large bowl until well
combined. Add parsley, shallot, vegetables and harissa
paste and season with salt and pepper. Stir to combine.

3 Pour mixture into prepared tin and smooth surface. Bake
for 25 minutes or until golden and set. Set aside to cool
for 5 minutes before cutting into squares to serve.

Cook's tips

* We used red onion, zucchini,
red capsicum and pumpkin
for the roasted vegetables.

* Store leftovers in an airtight
container in the fridge for up to
3 days. Enjoy cold or reheat in
microwave, if preferred.

Spinach and dill dip

 2 0 0 SmartPoints value per serve

PREP 10 MIN / SERVES 8

300 g silken firm tofu, drained
250 g frozen spinach, thawed
1 garlic clove, crushed
3 teaspoons finely chopped dill

1 Wrap tofu in paper towel and place a plate on top as a weight. Set aside for 5 minutes to drain. Discard paper.

2 Meanwhile, drain spinach and squeeze out excess moisture. Process tofu, spinach, garlic and dill in a food processor until almost smooth. Season with salt and pepper and serve.

Cook's tips

* To squeeze excess moisture from spinach, use your hands or place spinach in a colander and press down with a bowl that fits snugly inside.

* For a change from the usual carrot, celery and cucumber sticks, try serving your favourite dips with snow peas, capsicum strips, cherry tomatoes or radishes.

Roasted beetroot dip

 0 0 0 SmartPoints value per serve

PREP 5 MIN / COOK 40 MIN / SERVES 18

750 g whole beetroot
¼ cup (60 g) 99% fat-free
   plain yoghurt
1 teaspoon chopped thyme

1 Preheat oven to 180°C. Wash beetroot and chop in half (see tip). Add beetroot to a baking paper-lined roasting tin and bake for 40 minutes or until tender. Allow to cool, then peel.

2 Add beetroot to a food processor and process until almost smooth. Add yoghurt and process to combine. Transfer to a serving bowl. Sprinkle with thyme and serve.

Cook's tips

* If beetroots are large, cut into quarters. All pieces should be similar in size for even roasting.

* Save time by using a 500 g packet whole cooked beetroot, available from the fresh produce department in major supermarkets.

* Serve with grissini bread sticks (contains gluten). Check your WW app for SmartPoints.

The WW Essential Guide to Healthy Eating

Pumpkin *yoghurt* hummus

 2 0 0 SmartPoints value per serve

PREP 10 MIN / **COOK** 10 MIN / **SERVES** 4

200 g pumpkin, chopped

400 g can chickpeas, drained and rinsed

1 teaspoon ground cumin

1 garlic clove, crushed

¼ cup (60 g) 99% fat-free plain yoghurt

1 tablespoon lemon juice

2 tablespoons chopped coriander

1   Boil, steam or microwave pumpkin until tender. Drain.

2   Process pumpkin, chickpeas, cumin, garlic, yoghurt and lemon juice in a food processor until smooth. Add coriander and pulse to combine. Season with salt and pepper.

Cook's tips

* Store leftover hummus in an airtight container in the fridge for up to 3 days.

* Serve with vegetable sticks and cherry tomatoes.

Tzatziki

 1 0 0 SmartPoints value per serve

PREP 10 MIN / **SERVES** 4

200 g 99% fat-free plain yoghurt

2 teaspoons dried mint

2 garlic cloves, crushed

2 teaspoons lemon juice

½ Lebanese cucumber, seeded and coarsely grated

1   Combine yoghurt, mint, garlic, lemon juice and cucumber in a bowl. Season with salt and pepper. Serve.

Cook's tips

* For an authentic Greek flavour, add 1–2 teaspoon chopped dill.

* Serve dip with vegetable sticks or your favourite gluten-free crackers. Check your WW app for SmartPoints.

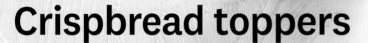

Crispbread toppers

Crispbread topped with beetroot dip and chicken

(3)(3)(3) **SmartPoints value per serve**

PREP 5 MIN / **SERVES** 1

1 rye crispbread

2 tablespoons beetroot dip

20 g Lebanese cucumber, cut into matchsticks

20 g cooked skinless chicken breast, shredded

1 teaspoon chopped dill

1   Spread crispbread with dip. Top with cucumber, chicken and dill.

Cook's tip

Use a store-bought beetroot dip or make your own on page 132.

Crispbread topped with onion dip and egg

(6)(5)(5) **SmartPoints value per serve**

PREP 5 MIN / **SERVES** 1

1 rye crispbread

2 tablespoons caramelised French onion dip

½ hard-boiled egg, sliced

1 teaspoon chopped chives

1   Spread crispbread with dip. Top with egg and sprinkle with chives. Season with salt and pepper.

Crispbread topped with capsicum dip

6 **6** **6** **SmartPoints value per serve**

PREP 5 MIN / **SERVES** 1

2 rye crispbreads
2 tablespoons spicy capsicum dip
½ cup (95 g) cherry tomato medley, quartered
3 pitted black olives, sliced
small handful of basil leaves

1 Spread crispbread with dip. Top with tomato, olives and basil.

Fig *and* pistachio trail mix

 SmartPoints value per serve

PREP 5 MIN / **COOK** 5 MIN + COOLING / **SERVES** 8

⅓ cup (45 g) pistachios

¼ cup (30 g) pecans, chopped

2 tablespoons pepitas
  (pumpkin seeds)

2 tablespoons sunflower seeds

2 tablespoons desiccated
  coconut

⅓ cup (50 g) dried
  cranberries, chopped

¼ cup (50 g) dried figs, chopped

1 Preheat oven to 180°C. Spread pistachios and pecans on a baking tray. Bake for 3 minutes. Stir. Add pepitas, sunflower seeds and coconut and bake for 2 minutes or until lightly browned. Cool for 10 minutes.

2 Combine nut mixture, cranberries and figs in a bowl. Cool completely before transferring to an airtight container.

Cook's tips

＊ Trail mix will keep for up to 2 weeks in an airtight container.

＊ To serve, pack individual portions into small containers or snap-lock bags ready for an on-the-go snack.

Popcorn

 SmartPoints value per serve

PREP 5 MIN / **COOK** 5 MIN / **SERVES** 4

80 g popcorn kernels

To cook the popcorn, place popcorn kernels in an air popper and cook following manufacturer's instructions. Alternatively, if you're using the microwave, place popcorn in a microwave-safe bowl, cover with plate and microwave on High (100%) for 3–4 minutes or until popping subsides. Be sure to lightly spray cooked popcorn with oil before adding flavour to help it stick.

Herb and garlic popcorn

 SmartPoints value per serve

PREP 5 MIN / **SERVES** 4

Combine 2 tablespoons each of chopped chives and flat-leaf parsley, 1 teaspoon chopped rosemary, 1 teaspoon lemon zest and ½ teaspoon garlic salt in a bowl. Sprinkle over popcorn and toss to combine. Serve.

Tex Mex popcorn

 SmartPoints value per serve

PREP 5 MIN / **SERVES** 4

Combine 1 teaspoon each of chilli powder, ground cumin and smoked paprika, ½ teaspoon garlic powder and ½ teaspoon salt in a small bowl. Sprinkle over popcorn and toss to combine. Serve.

Kale and lemon popcorn

 SmartPoints value per serve

PREP 5 MIN / **COOK** 10 MIN
SERVES 4

Preheat oven to 160°C. Spread 4 handfuls of chopped kale on a baking tray and lightly spray with oil. Bake for 8–10 minutes or until crisp. Process in a food processor with 2 teaspoons lemon zest. Sprinkle over popcorn and toss to combine. Serve.

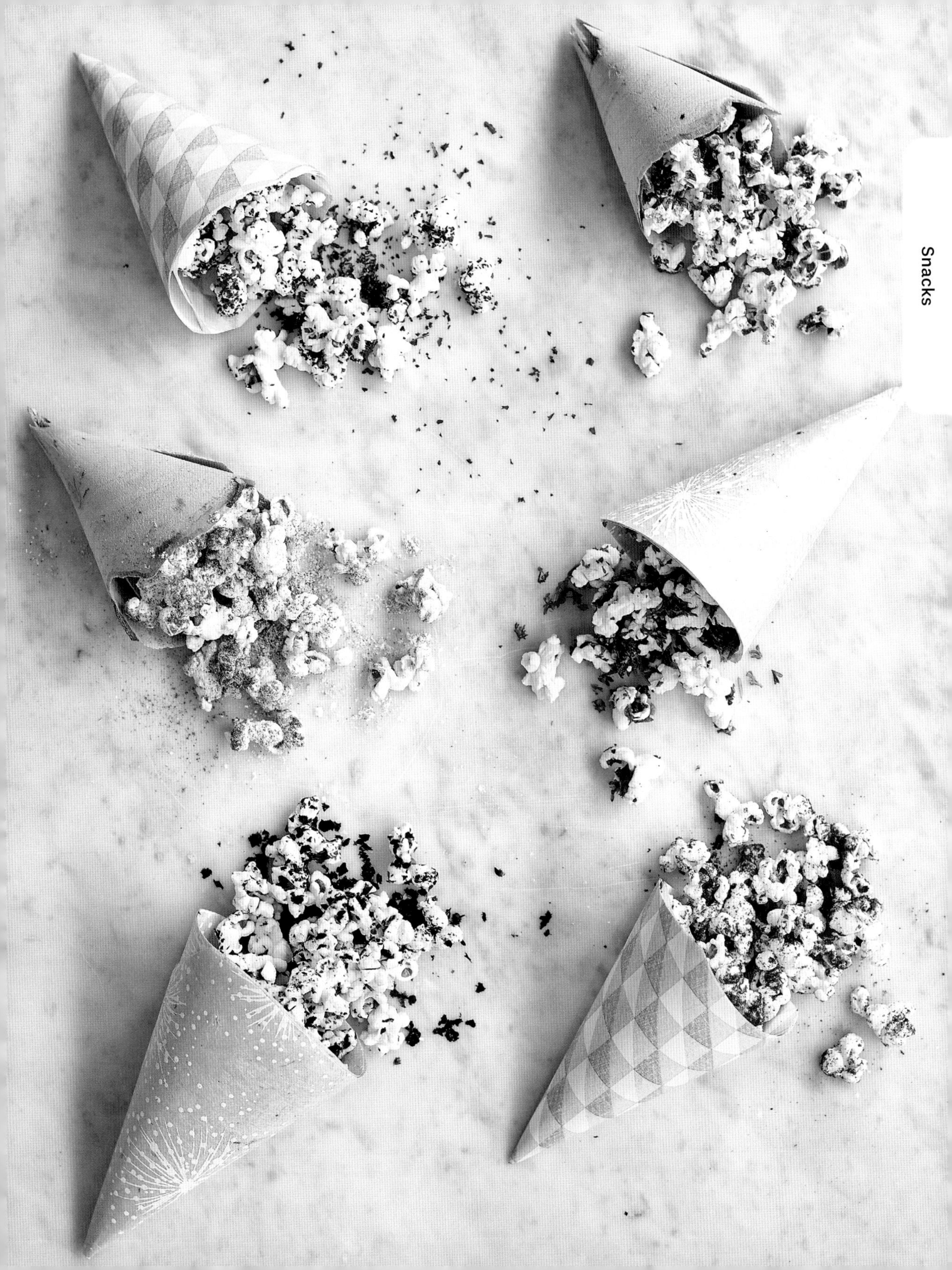

Coconut *and* date muesli bars

4 **4** **3**   **SmartPoints value per serve**

PREP 15 MIN / **COOK** 10 MIN + COOLING / **SERVES** 24

⅔ cup (160 g) 99% fat-free
   plain yoghurt

½ cup (110 g) brown sugar

2 eggs

10 medjool dates, pitted
   and finely chopped

¾ cup (115 g) wholemeal flour

½ cup (50 g) wheat germ

1 teaspoon bicarbonate of soda

2¾ cups (250 g) rolled oats

¼ cup (40 g) linseeds or
   flaxseeds

¾ cup (60 g) desiccated coconut

1   Preheat oven to 200°C. Lightly spray a 25 cm x 35 cm rectangular slice tin with oil. Line base and sides with baking paper, extending paper 4 cm above edges.

2   Whisk yoghurt, sugar and eggs in a large bowl until combined. Stir in dates. Combine flour, wheat germ and bicarbonate of soda in a bowl. Stir flour mixture into egg mixture until combined. Add oats, linseeds and coconut, and mix well.

3   Transfer mixture to the prepared tin and level the surface with the back of a spoon. Bake for 8 minutes or until golden brown. Transfer to a wire rack to cool. Cut into 24 rectangles to serve.

Cook's tip

Store in an airtight container in the fridge for up to 5 days.

Smoked *salmon* sushi slice

 SmartPoints value per serve

PREP 20 MIN / **COOK** 20 MIN + CHILLING / **SERVES** 24

1 cup (200 g) sushi rice (see tip)

2 tablespoons rice wine vinegar

2 teaspoons caster sugar

100 g smoked salmon slices

3 teaspoons wasabi paste

50 g snow pea sprouts

1 tablespoon pickled ginger,
    drained and thinly sliced

1 Cook rice following packet instructions until just tender. Place rice in a large glass or wooden bowl. Stir vinegar, sugar and ½ teaspoon salt in a small bowl until sugar has dissolved. Using a large, flat wooden spoon or plastic spatula, gradually stir vinegar mixture into rice, lifting and turning rice continuously until almost cool. Cover rice with a damp cloth.

2 Line base and sides of a 20 cm (base measurement) square cake tin with plastic wrap. Arrange salmon in a single layer over base of tin, trimming to fit. Spread salmon with wasabi paste. Using damp hands, press rice evenly over salmon. Cover and place in fridge for 1 hour.

3 Invert sushi onto a chopping board. Remove and discard plastic wrap. Cut into 24 pieces. Top each slice with sprouts and pickled ginger to serve.

Cook's tip

If you can't find sushi rice at your supermarket, substitute with arborio rice.

Easy sausage rolls

2 **2** **2** SmartPoints value per serve

PREP 15 MIN / COOK 15 MIN / SERVES 24

2 sheets reduced-fat puff
   pastry, just thawed
8 x 75 g extra-lean
   pork sausages
1 egg, lightly beaten
1 teaspoon sesame seeds

1   Preheat oven to 200°C. Line a large baking tray with baking paper. Cut pastry sheets into quarters to give 8 even-sized squares.

2   Place a sausage in the centre of each pastry square. Brush edges of pastry with a little egg. Roll pastry to enclose sausages. Trim any excess pastry at the ends. Arrange rolls, seam-side down, on prepared tray. Brush with egg and sprinkle with sesame seeds.

3   Bake for 12–15 minutes or until pastry is golden brown and sausages are cooked through. Cool slightly. Using a serrated knife, cut each sausage roll into 3 pieces. Serve warm.

Cook's tip

Serve with ¼ cup (60 ml) tomato sauce for dipping. Check your WW app for SmartPoints.

The WW Essential Guide to Healthy Eating

Lunch

Zero vegie soup

 0 **0** **0** SmartPoints value per serve

PREP 15 MIN / **COOK** 20 MIN / **SERVES** 6

2 gluten-free vegetable
   stock cubes

1 onion, coarsely chopped

2 garlic cloves, finely chopped

2 celery sticks, sliced

2 carrots, cut into 1 cm pieces

2 zucchini, cut into 1 cm pieces

1 red capsicum, cut into
   1.5 cm pieces

2 x 400 g cans chopped
   tomatoes

½ cup shredded basil

⅓ cup shredded
   flat-leaf parsley

1 Combine stock cubes with 4 cups (1 litre) boiling water
   in a large jug.

2 Place onion, garlic, celery, carrot, zucchini, capsicum,
   tomatoes and stock in a large saucepan over high heat.
   Bring to the boil.

3 Reduce heat and simmer, uncovered, for 15 minutes
   or until vegetables are tender.

4 Add basil and parsley and stir to combine.

Cook's tip

To peel garlic, cover the cloves with
the flat side of a large knife. Press
down with the heel of your hand until
the clove splits, then pull off the skin.

Pumpkin *soup*

  SmartPoints value per serve

PREP 5 MIN / **COOK** 5 MIN / **SERVES** 4

750 g roasted pumpkin (see tip)

700 ml vegetable stock,
    made with 2 gluten-free
    stock cubes

1 tablespoon 99% fat-free
    plain yoghurt

1   Process pumpkin with stock in a food processor
    until smooth.

2   Transfer to a saucepan and stir over medium heat until
    hot, adding a little water if consistency is too thick.
    Season with salt. Divide among four bowls. Serve with
    a swirl of yoghurt and a sprinkle of pepper.

Cook's tip

For 750 g roasted pumpkin, spread
about 1.2 kg peeled, chopped pumpkin
over a baking paper-lined baking tray
or roasting tin and lightly spray with
oil. Bake at 200°C for 25–30 minutes,
or until tender. For extra flavour, lightly
sprinkle with your favourite seasoning
blend such as Moroccan, Cajun
or Tuscan before baking.

The WW Essential Guide to Healthy Eating

Sweet potato *and* chickpea patties

 SmartPoints value per serve

PREP 10 MIN / **COOK** 25 MIN / **SERVES** 4

500 g sweet potato (kumara),
   coarsely chopped

1 tablespoon korma curry paste

400 g can chickpeas, drained
   and rinsed

100 g frozen sliced green beans,
   thawed, chopped

2 green shallots (spring onions),
   thinly sliced

¼ cup finely chopped coriander

1 egg, lightly beaten

⅓ cup (50 g) plain flour

1 tablespoon olive oil

2 tablespoons shredded mint

½ cup (120 g) 99% fat-free
   plain yoghurt

lime halves, to serve

1   Boil, steam or microwave sweet potato until just tender. Drain. Place in a bowl and mash until smooth. Stir in curry paste. Cool for 5 minutes.

2   Place chickpeas in a small bowl and roughly mash. Add chickpeas, beans, shallot, coriander, egg and flour to potato and mix well. Season with salt and pepper.

3   Heat half the oil in a large non-stick frying pan over medium–high heat. Spoon six ¼-cup measures of potato mixture into the pan and flatten to 1 cm thick. Cook for 2–3 minutes each side or until evenly browned. Transfer to a baking paper-lined baking tray and keep warm in a 150°C oven while cooking the second batch. Repeat with remaining oil and potato mixture to make 12 patties.

4   Combine mint and yoghurt in a small bowl. Season with salt and pepper. Serve patties with mint yoghurt and lime halves.

Serve with mixed-leaf green salad.

The WW Essential Guide to Healthy Eating

Thai chicken *and* coconut soup

 SmartPoints value per serve

PREP 5 MIN / **COOK** 10 MIN / **SERVES** 4

2 tablespoons Thai red
   curry paste

¾ cup (180 ml) light coconut milk

2 x 28 g chicken stock pots
   (see tip)

80 g rice vermicelli
   noodles, broken

250 g frozen Thai stir-fry
   vegetables (see tip)

1 bunch baby choy sum, chopped

200 g cooked skinless chicken
   breast, chopped

1 tablespoon lime juice

½ cup coriander leaves

1   Lightly spray a large saucepan with oil and heat over medium–high heat. Cook paste, stirring, for 1–2 minutes or until fragrant. Add coconut milk and bring to the boil.

2   Add stock pots and 4 cups (1 litre) boiling water and bring to the boil. Add noodles and boil, covered, for 2 minutes.

3   Add frozen vegetables and reduce heat. Simmer, uncovered, for 2 minutes. Add choy sum, chicken and juice and simmer, uncovered, for a further 2–3 minutes or until vegies are just tender. Sprinkle with coriander leaves to serve.

Cook's tips

* Stock pots are small containers of concentrated liquid stock available at most major supermarkets. If unavailable, use stock cubes or powder to make 4 cups (1 litre) stock.
* We used a frozen stir-fry mix consisting of carrot, baby corn, green beans and broccoli but you can use any frozen stir-fry mix.
* To get more juice from a lime, roll it back and forth on the bench a few times while pressing down firmly with your hand before cutting it in half.

Spicy vegetarian chickpea *and* vegie bowl

 SmartPoints value per serve

PREP 15 MIN / **COOK** 30 MIN / **SERVES** 4

½ red onion, finely chopped

2 celery sticks, finely chopped

1 carrot, finely chopped

2 garlic cloves, crushed

1 teaspoon finely grated ginger

1 tablespoon Moroccan seasoning
(see tip)

1½ cups (420 g) tomato puree

400 g can chickpeas, drained
and rinsed

1 zucchini, cut into 1 cm pieces

100 g green beans, cut into
1 cm pieces

4 cups (120 g) mixed salad leaves

1 small avocado, thinly sliced

1 tablespoon black sesame seeds

1   Lightly spray a large non-stick saucepan with oil and heat over medium–high heat. Cook onion, celery and carrot, stirring, for 5 minutes or until onion has softened. Add garlic and ginger and cook, stirring, for 1 minute.

2   Add Moroccan seasoning and cook, stirring, for 1 minute or until fragrant. Stir in tomato puree and ¾ cup (185 ml) water and bring to the boil. Reduce heat and simmer, covered, for 10 minutes.

3   Add chickpeas, zucchini and beans and simmer, uncovered, for 8–10 minutes or until vegetables are tender. Serve with salad leaves and avocado sprinkled with black sesame seeds.

Cook's tips

* You could swap the Moroccan seasoning with 2 teaspoons ground cumin, 1 teaspoon ground coriander, 1 teaspoon chilli flakes and 1 teaspoon paprika.
* Serve with 1½ cups of cooked brown rice. Check your WW app for SmartPoints.

The WW Essential Guide to Healthy Eating

Warm Greek lamb salad *with* mint pesto

 SmartPoints value per serve

PREP 30 MIN / **COOK** 10 MIN / **SERVES** 4

2 teaspoons lemon zest

1 teaspoon dried oregano

2 garlic cloves, crushed

500 g lean lamb backstrap,
    fat trimmed

1 bunch mint, leaves picked

2 tablespoons lemon juice

1 tablespoon olive oil

1 tablespoon slivered almonds,
    toasted (see tip)

2 red capsicums, cut into
    3 cm wide strips

80 g baby rocket

250 g cherry tomatoes, halved

⅓ cup (50 g) black olives

80 g reduced-fat feta, crumbled

lemon wedges, to serve

1   Combine lemon zest, oregano and half the garlic in a baking dish. Add lamb and turn to coat. Cover and set aside in the fridge.

2   To make pesto, process mint, lemon juice, oil, almonds and remaining garlic in a food processor until a paste forms. Transfer to a bowl, cover and set aside.

3   Preheat a chargrill or barbecue grill on medium heat. Cook capsicum, turning, for 10 minutes until tender and lightly charred.

4   Meanwhile, lightly spray lamb with oil and grill for 4 minutes each side or until cooked to your liking. Transfer to a plate. Cover lamb with foil and set aside to rest for 5 minutes before slicing thinly.

5   Combine rocket, capsicum and tomato on a platter. Top with lamb, olives and feta. Dollop with pesto and serve with lemon wedges.

Cook's tips

* To serve with garlic bread (contains gluten), grill 4 x 40 g slices sourdough bread for 1–2 minutes each side or until golden. While still warm, rub 1 side of each slice with the cut side of 1 garlic clove (halved). Check your WW app for SmartPoints.

* To toast almonds, heat a small non-stick frying pan over medium heat. Cook almonds, stirring, for 2–3 minutes or until light golden.

Asian-style *chicken* omelettes

 SmartPoints value per serve

PREP 10 MIN / **COOK** 15 MIN / **SERVES** 4

200 g shredded carrot (see tip)

150 g snow peas, trimmed, thinly sliced

2 cups (320 g) shredded cooked skinless chicken breast

80 g alfalfa sprouts (see tip)

3 green shallots (spring onions), thinly sliced

8 eggs

2 teaspoons soy sauce

1 tablespoon oyster sauce

coriander sprigs, to garnish

1 Combine carrot, snow peas, chicken, sprouts and two-thirds of the shallot in a bowl.

2 Whisk eggs and soy sauce in a jug until well combined.

3 Lightly spray a non-stick frying pan with oil and heat over medium–high heat. Pour one-quarter of the egg mixture into pan and cook for 30 seconds or until base of omelette starts to set. Using a spatula, draw edges of omelette into the centre to allow uncooked egg to run underneath. Continue doing this until egg is nearly set.

4 Place one-quarter of the carrot mixture over half the omelette. Fold unfilled half of omelette over filling to enclose. Slide onto a plate. Cover to keep warm. Repeat with remaining egg mixture and carrot filling to make three more omelettes. Drizzle with oyster sauce and sprinkle with remaining shallot and coriander to serve.

Cook's tips

* Packets of shredded carrot are available in the fresh produce section of most supermarkets. If unavailable, use 2 medium carrots, coarsely grated.

* You can substitute snow pea sprouts for alfalfa sprouts.

* Serve with steamed Asian greens such as bok choy or choy sum.

Cheat's quiche Lorraine

 SmartPoints value per serve

PREP 15 MIN / **COOK** 55 MIN / **SERVES** 4

3 x 48 g wholemeal tortillas

1 tablespoon sunflower oil

1 onion, thinly sliced

125 g short-cut bacon,
   coarsely chopped

4 eggs

2 tablespoons finely chopped
   flat-leaf parsley

100 ml vegetable stock made
   with ¼ stock cube

50 g grated reduced-fat
   cheddar cheese

1   Preheat oven to 180°C and heat a baking tray until hot. Brush one side of the tortillas with 2 teaspoons oil, then microwave each on High (100%) for 10 seconds to soften. Press one tortilla, oil-side down, into base of a 20 cm round cake tin or pie dish. Halve two remaining tortillas and press around side of tin, making sure they overlap and leave no gaps.

2   Heat remaining oil in a non-stick frying pan over medium heat. Cook onion, stirring, for 5 minutes, or until softened. Add bacon and cook for 3 minutes, or until lightly browned.

3   In a bowl, lightly whisk eggs, parsley and stock. Season with pepper.

4   Scatter two-thirds of the cheese over tortillas in prepared tin or dish. Spoon over onion mixture. Pour over egg mixture then top with remaining cheese. Transfer to hot baking tray and bake for 40–45 minutes, or until filling is set.

5   Cool in tin or dish for 10 minutes. Cut into wedges to serve.

The WW Essential Guide to Healthy Eating

Vietnamese chicken salad

 SmartPoints value per serve

5 4 4

PREP 15 MIN / **COOK** 15 MIN / **SERVES** 4

100 g dried rice noodles

450 g skinless chicken breast
(see tip)

300 g wombok (Chinese
cabbage), finely shredded

1 carrot, cut into matchsticks

½ cup chopped coriander

¼ cup chopped mint

1 long red chilli, seeded and
thinly sliced

¼ cup (60 ml) lime juice

2 tablespoons fish sauce

1 tablespoon brown sugar

1 tablespoon unsalted roasted
peanuts, chopped

1 Prepare rice noodles following packet instructions. Rinse under cold water, then drain. Using kitchen scissors, roughly cut rice noodles into shorter lengths and place in a large bowl.

2 Place chicken in a saucepan of boiling water. Reduce heat and simmer, uncovered, for 8–10 minutes or until chicken is cooked through. Drain, set aside to cool, then shred chicken coarsely.

3 Add chicken, wombok, carrot, coriander, mint and chilli to noodles. Whisk lime juice, fish sauce and sugar in a small bowl, then drizzle over chicken salad and toss gently until combined. Serve sprinkled with peanuts.

Cook's tip

Chicken can be cooked and shredded 1 day ahead. Keep in a container in the fridge until ready to assemble salad.

Chicken, leek *and* rice soup

 SmartPoints value per serve

PREP 15 MIN / **COOK** 45 MIN / **SERVES** 4

2 teaspoons olive oil

1 leek, white part only, thinly sliced

1 carrot, finely chopped

2 celery sticks, finely chopped

450 g skinless chicken thigh fillets, fat trimmed, cut into 2 cm pieces

2 garlic cloves, crushed

4 cups (1 litre) reduced-salt chicken stock

⅓ cup (65 g) brown rice

1 zucchini, cut into 2 cm pieces

150 g green beans, cut into 3 cm pieces

2 tablespoons chopped flat-leaf parsley

1 Heat oil in a saucepan over medium heat. Cook leek, carrot and celery, stirring, for 5 minutes or until softened.

2 Add chicken and cook, stirring, for 3–4 minutes or until browned. Add garlic and cook, stirring, for 30 seconds or until fragrant. Stir in stock and rice and bring to the boil. Reduce heat and simmer, partially covered, stirring occasionally, for 30 minutes or until rice is tender.

3 Stir in zucchini and beans and simmer, uncovered, for 2–3 minutes or until vegetables are just tender. Season with salt and pepper. Serve sprinkled with parsley.

Cook's tip

Keep leftover soup in a container in the fridge for up to 2 days. To serve, reheat in microwave, or in a small saucepan on stovetop until hot.

The WW Essential Guide to Healthy Eating

Grilled vegie salad

 SmartPoints value per serve

PREP 20 MIN / **COOK** 20 MIN / **SERVES** 8

3 yellow capsicums, quartered

1 eggplant, thinly sliced
   lengthways

3 zucchini, thinly sliced
   lengthways

200 g grape tomatoes, halved

⅓ cup (80 g) 99% fat-free
   plain yoghurt

1 tablespoon lemon juice

1 garlic clove, crushed

2 teaspoons tahini

¼ teaspoon ground cumin

¼ cup chopped flat-leaf parsley

seeds of 1 pomegranate

1   Preheat a grill on high and line the grill tray with foil. Place capsicum, skin-side up, on the prepared tray and cook under the grill for 8 minutes or until the skin blackens. Transfer to a large bowl. Cover and set aside.

2   Lightly spray both sides of the eggplant slices with olive oil. Arrange eggplant, in a single layer, on the foil-lined grill tray and cook under the grill for 4 minutes each side or until browned and tender. Transfer to a plate and cover to keep warm. Lightly spray zucchini and tomato with oil and grill for 4 minutes or until tender.

3   Meanwhile, to make dressing, place yoghurt, lemon juice, garlic, tahini, cumin and 2 teaspoons water in a small bowl. Season with salt and pepper and whisk to combine.

4   Peel capsicum, discard skin and cut flesh into thick strips. Arrange capsicum, eggplant and zucchini on a platter. Top with tomato and half the parsley. Drizzle with dressing and sprinkle with remaining parsley and pomegranate seeds.

Cook's tips

* Substitute red capsicums if yellow capsicums are unavailable.

* For a shortcut, replace whole pomegranate with a punnet of pomegranate seeds (arils), available from the fresh produce section of major supermarkets.

The WW Essential Guide to Healthy Eating

Salmon pan eggs

  SmartPoints value per serve

PREP 5 MIN / **COOK** 20 MIN / **SERVES** 8

10 eggs, lightly beaten

¼ cup (60 ml) skim milk

200 g superfood vegetable mix
(see tips)

415 g can red salmon in spring
water, drained, skin
removed, flaked

1   Preheat oven to 200°C. Lightly spray a shallow
30 cm x 20 cm (base measurement) baking dish with oil
and line base and sides with baking paper.

2   Whisk eggs and milk in a large bowl until combined.
Season with salt and pepper and stir through vegetables.
Pour mixture into prepared dish. Top with salmon and
bake for 18–20 minutes or until set.

3   Using baking paper lining, transfer pan eggs to a chopping
board and cut into 8 slices to serve.

Cook's tips

* Superfood vegetable mix is a mix of
  shredded carrot, cabbage, beetroot,
  kale, daikon radish and celery. If
  unavailable, replace with undressed
  coleslaw mix.
* Leftover pan eggs will keep for
  up to 2 days in a container in the
  fridge. Reheat individual slices
  in a microwave on High (100%)
  in 15 seconds bursts until hot.
* Serve with a leafy green salad.

The WW Essential Guide to Healthy Eating

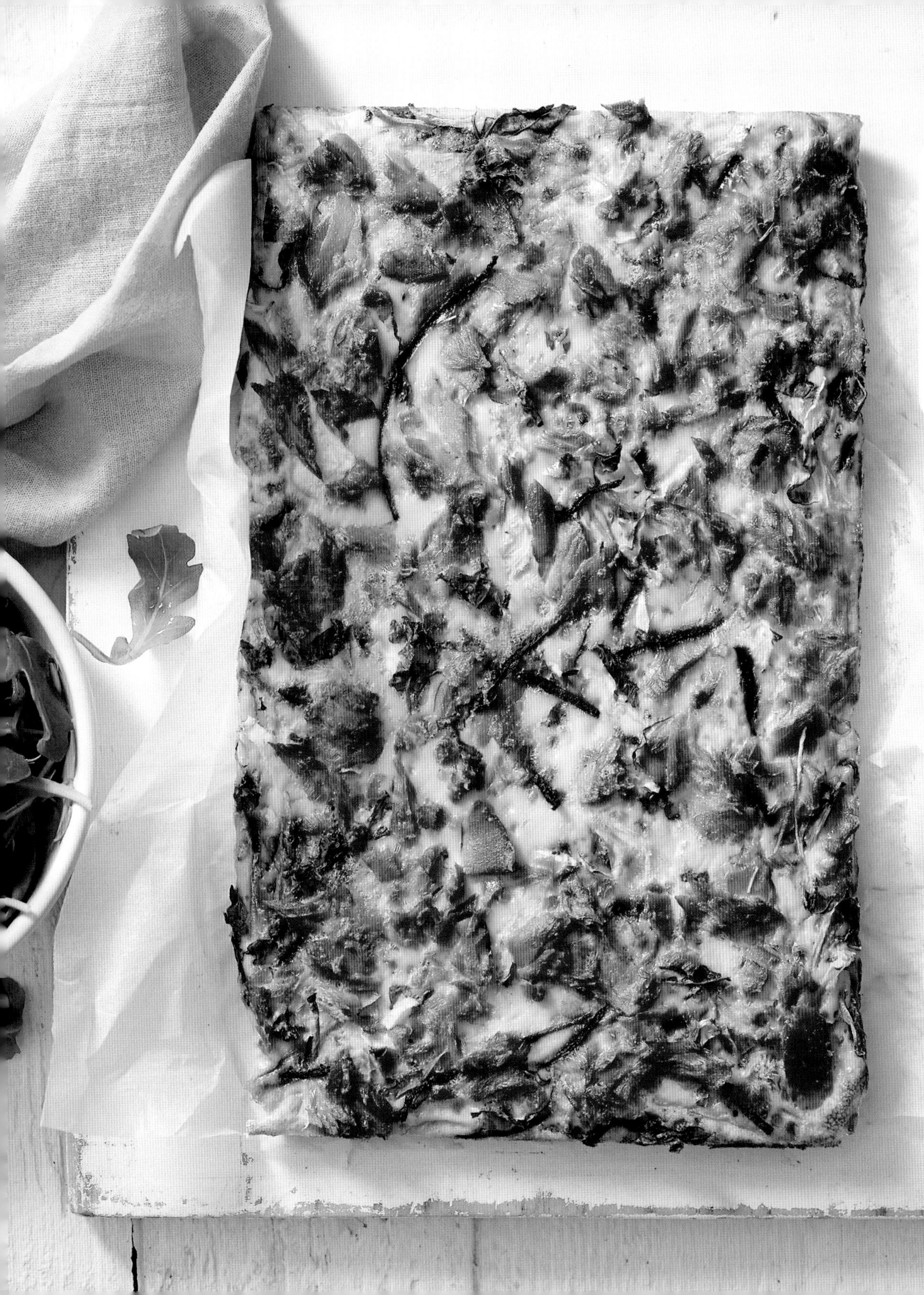

Hearty steak sandwiches

 SmartPoints value per serve

PREP 5 MIN / **COOK** 10 MIN / **SERVES** 4

1 red onion, sliced

2 tablespoons lemon juice

8 x 35 g slices sourdough bread

8 x 65 g beef sizzle steaks
    (see tip)

80 g mixed salad leaves

2 Lebanese cucumbers, sliced

2 tomatoes, sliced

2 tablespoons tomato relish

1. Combine onion and lemon juice in a small bowl, set aside to marinate for 10 minutes.

2. Lightly spray a chargrill or barbecue with oil and heat on high. Cook bread for 2 minutes each side or until charred and golden. Cook steaks for 1 minute each side or until just charred.

3. Drain onion mixture on paper towel. Top four pieces of bread with salad leaves, steaks, cucumber, tomato and onion mixture. Top with relish and sandwich with remaining bread to serve.

Cook's tip

Sizzle steaks are thin, tenderised steaks. They are available from the refrigerated meat cabinets of most supermarkets. If unavailable you can use minute steaks.

The WW Essential Guide to Healthy Eating

Easy beef burger

 SmartPoints value per serve

PREP 10 MIN / **COOK** 10 MIN / **SERVES** 4

500 g extra-lean beef mince

1 red onion, half finely chopped,
    half thinly sliced

1 egg, lightly beaten

8 butter lettuce leaves

1 tomato, thinly sliced

2 pickled gherkins, thinly sliced

4 x 50 g wholemeal bread rolls,
    split in half

1   Combine mince, finely chopped onion and egg in a bowl. Shape mixture into four 2 cm-thick patties. Season with salt and pepper.

2   Lightly spray a large non-stick frying pan or chargrill pan with oil and heat over medium heat. Cook patties for 10 minutes, turning occasionally, or until cooked through.

3   Layer lettuce, tomato, burger patties, sliced onion and gherkins over roll bases. Cover with roll tops to serve.

For added flavour, spread 1 teaspoon
tomato sauce over each burger patty.

The WW Essential Guide to Healthy Eating

Chicken *and* vegie rice paper rolls

 SmartPoints value per serve

PREP 20 MIN / **COOK** 10 MIN / **SERVES** 4

50 g vermicelli noodles

100 g cooked skinless chicken
   breast, shredded

60 g snow peas, trimmed and
   thinly sliced

½ carrot, cut into matchsticks

8 x 10 g rice paper roll wrappers

8 mint leaves

8 coriander sprigs

1   Prepare noodles following packet instructions, until just tender. Rinse under cold water. Drain. Using scissors, roughly cut noodles into shorter lengths. Place noodles in a large bowl with the chicken, snow peas and carrot. Toss to combine.

2   Working with one wrapper at a time, dip rice paper in a shallow dish of warm water for 10–20 seconds or until just softened. Lay on a clean tea towel to absorb excess water. Place one-eighth of the noodle mixture across the centre of the wrapper. Top with a mint leaf and a coriander sprig.

3   Fold in left and right edges of wrapper, then starting from the bottom, roll up to enclose filling. Place roll on a serving plate and cover with a slightly damp clean cloth to stop it from drying out. Repeat with remaining rice paper and filling to make 8 rolls.

Cook's tips

* Serve with sweet chilli sauce.
  Check your WW app for the
  SmartPoints.

* Filling can be made several
  hours ahead. Keep in a container
  in the fridge. Prepare rolls just
  before serving.

Greek-style *lamb* wraps

7 **7** **7** SmartPoints value per serve

PREP 15 MIN / **COOK** 10 MIN / **SERVES** 4

400 g lean lamb backstrap,
   fat trimmed

4 x 45 g soft white wraps

60 g rocket and baby
   spinach mix

250 g cherry tomatoes,
   quartered

⅓ cup (90 g) low-fat tzatziki
   (see page 128)

1   Preheat a chargrill or barbecue on medium–high. Lightly spray lamb with oil and season with salt and pepper. Cook lamb for 3–4 minutes each side or until cooked to your liking. Transfer to a plate. Cover with foil and set aside for 5 minutes to rest before slicing thinly.

2   Heat wraps following packet instructions. Divide rocket and spinach mix and tomato among wraps. Top with lamb and tzatziki. Roll up to enclose filling.

Replace lamb with skinless chicken breast, if preferred. Cook chicken for about 5 minutes each side, or until cooked through. Check your WW app for the SmartPoints.

The WW Essential Guide to Healthy Eating

Sweet potato, spinach *and* chickpea buddha bowl

 SmartPoints value per serve

PREP 10 MIN / **COOK** 20 MIN / **SERVES** 2

300 g sweet potato (kumara), chopped

⅓ cup (80 g) 99% fat-free plain yoghurt

1 tablespoon tahini

1 tablespoon lemon juice

1 teaspoon olive oil

1 onion, finely chopped

1 garlic clove, crushed

125 g canned chickpeas, rinsed, drained

3 teaspoons Moroccan seasoning

60 g baby spinach leaves

½ teaspoon sesame seeds, toasted (see tips)

1 Boil, steam or microwave sweet potato until just tender. Drain and set aside to cool.

2 Meanwhile, combine yoghurt, tahini and lemon juice in a small bowl. Season with salt and pepper.

3 Heat oil in a large non-stick frying pan over medium heat. Cook onion and garlic, stirring, for 3–4 minutes or until softened. Add chickpeas and Moroccan seasoning and cook, stirring, for 2 minutes.

4 Add sweet potato and cook, tossing gently, for 2–3 minutes or until light golden. Add spinach and cook, covered, for 2 minutes or until wilted. Spoon mixture into two bowls. Top with tahini yoghurt and sprinkle with sesame seeds to serve.

Cook's tips

* To toast sesame seeds, toss them in a small non-stick frying pan over medium heat until golden.

* Store leftovers in an airtight container in the fridge, with dressing and sesame seeds in separate containers. Reheat potato mixture in the microwave to serve.

Fish *and* chips

6 **4** **3** SmartPoints value per serve

PREP 25 MIN / COOK 50 MIN / SERVES 8

4 x 150 g coliban potatoes,
   cut into 1 cm-thick chips
600 g firm white fish (see tips)
2 tablespoons plain flour
80 g panko breadcrumbs
⅓ cup finely chopped
   flat-leaf parsley
2 teaspoons lemon zest
1 egg, lightly beaten
½ cup (120 g) 99% fat-free
   plain yoghurt
2 tablespoons light whole-egg
   mayonnaise
2 tablespoons baby capers,
   rinsed, drained and
   finely chopped
2 tablespoons (30 g) finely
   chopped gherkins
2 tablespoons finely
   chopped dill
lemon cheeks or wedges,
   to serve

1 Preheat oven to 200°C. Line two large baking trays with baking paper. Spread potato chips in a single layer over a prepared tray. Lightly spray with oil and season with salt and pepper. Bake for 30 minutes.

2 Meanwhile, cut the fish into 4 cm-wide, 8–10 cm-long strips. Place flour on a large plate and season with salt and pepper. Combine the breadcrumbs, 2 tablespoons parsley and lemon zest in a shallow bowl. Dip fish, one piece at a time, into flour to lightly coat, shake off excess. Dip into egg, then into breadcrumb mixture to coat. Arrange in a single layer over remaining prepared tray. Lightly spray with oil.

3 Remove chips from oven and turn. Return chips to oven with fish. Bake for about 20 minutes or until fish is golden and cooked through and chips are crisp and golden, turning fish halfway during cooking time.

4 To make the tartare sauce, combine yoghurt, mayonnaise, capers, gherkins, dill and remaining parsley in a small bowl. Season with salt and pepper. Serve with fish and chips and lemon cheeks or wedges.

Cook's tips

* Use any boneless firm, white fish for this recipe. Try ling, snapper or dory.
* For crispiest results, it's important for chips and fish to be well spread out on trays. If your baking trays are smaller, use an extra tray for more space.

Dinner

Sarah's *easy* pasta bake

④ ④ ④ **SmartPoints value per serve**

PREP 15 MIN / **COOK** 45 MIN / **SERVES** 6

1 teaspoon olive oil

1 onion, coarsely grated

3 garlic cloves, crushed

2 carrots, coarsely grated

1 zucchini, coarsely grated

240 g turkey breast mince
  (see tips)

400 g can diced tomatoes

145 g dried elbow pasta

2 teaspoons finely chopped
  thyme, plus extra sprigs
  to garnish

½ cup (60 g) grated mozzarella

1 Preheat oven to 180°C. Heat oil in a large saucepan over medium–high heat. Cook onion, garlic, carrot and zucchini, stirring, for 5 minutes or until soft. Add mince and cook, breaking up any lumps, for 5 minutes or until mince has browned.

2 Add tomatoes. Fill tomato can three-quarters full with water and add to pan. Season with salt and pepper. Stir in pasta and thyme until well combined.

3 Transfer pasta mixture to a 8-cup (2 litre) capacity baking dish and sprinkle with mozzarella. Bake for 35 minutes or until cheese is golden and bubbling and pasta is tender. Stand for 5 minutes. Serve sprinkled with extra thyme sprigs.

Cook's tip

* You can use chicken breast mince instead of turkey breast mince for the same SmartPoints.

* Traditional pasta bake recipes can be up to 25 SmartPoints per serve. WW's version of this classic is healthier by using less oil, less cheese and a tomato-based sauce.

Member recipe
by Sarah Van Dyke
Find more of Sarah's recipes
@sarahs_recipes

Beef mince chow mein

9 **9** **9** **SmartPoints value per serve**

PREP 20 MIN / **COOK** 30 MIN / **SERVES** 4

500 g lean beef mince (see tips)

1 onion, finely chopped

1 tablespoon mild curry powder

1 carrot, grated

¼ small white (savoy) cabbage,
   finely shredded

2 celery sticks, finely chopped

2 tablespoons white
   long-grain rice

2 x 40 g packets reduced-salt
   chicken noodle soup mix

2 tablespoons soy sauce

150 g frozen sliced green beans

1   Lightly spray a large saucepan with oil and heat over high heat. Add mince and onion. Cook, breaking up any lumps, for 6–8 minutes or until mince has browned.

2   Add curry powder and cook, stirring, for 1 minute or until fragrant. Add carrot, cabbage, celery, rice, soup mix, soy sauce and 2 cups (500 ml) water and bring to the boil. Reduce heat and simmer, covered, for 20 minutes or until water is absorbed and rice is tender. Add beans for the last 2 minutes of cooking. Serve.

Cook's tips

* Serve with ZeroPoints steamed Asian greens, such as baby bok choy or choy sum.
* You can use lean chicken mince instead of beef. Check your WW app for the SmartPoints.

Almond chicken schnitzel *with* tangy coleslaw

 SmartPoints value per serve

PREP 20 MIN / **COOK** 10 MIN / **SERVES** 4

105 g panko breadcrumbs

¼ cup (30 g) almond meal

4 x 150 g skinless chicken breasts

¼ teaspoon chilli powder

1 egg, lightly beaten

1 tablespoon olive oil

2 tablespoons lime juice

1 cup (85 g) shredded
   red cabbage

½ cup coriander leaves

lime wedges, to serve

1 Combine panko breadcrumbs and almond meal on a sheet of baking paper. Sprinkle chicken with ½ teaspoon salt and chilli powder. Dip chicken, one at a time, in egg, then coat with panko mixture.

2 Heat 2 teaspoons oil in a large non-stick frying pan over medium heat. Add chicken and cook for 3–4 minutes on each side or until chicken is browned and cooked through.

3 Meanwhile, in a bowl, combine lime juice and remaining oil and season with salt and pepper. Add cabbage and coriander and toss to coat. Serve chicken with slaw and lime wedges.

Chinese *chicken* rissoles

  SmartPoints value per serve

PREP 10 MIN / **COOK** 15 MIN / **SERVES** 4

500 g chicken breast mince

2 tablespoons soy sauce

3 teaspoons finely grated ginger

2 teaspoons minced garlic

3 green shallots (spring onions),
   finely sliced

1 egg, lightly beaten

1   Combine mince, 1 tablespoon soy sauce, 2 teaspoons ginger, garlic, shallot and egg in a bowl.

2   Divide mixture into 12 equal portions. Using slightly damp hands, shape portions into patties about 2 cm thick.

3   Line a large non-stick frying pan with a round of baking paper and heat over medium heat. Cook rissoles, in two batches, for 3 minutes each side or until browned and cooked through.

4   Meanwhile, combine remaining soy and ginger in a small dish. Serve rissoles with dipping sauce.

Cook's tip

Serve with ½ cup (85 g) steamed brown rice and stir-fried snow peas and red capsicum. Check your WW app for additional SmartPoints.

The WW Essential Guide to Healthy Eating

One-pot chilli chicken *and* bean bowl

 SmartPoints value per serve

PREP 10 MIN / **COOK** 15 MIN / **SERVES** 4

1 red onion, finely chopped

2 teaspoons Mexican chilli
   powder

400 g can diced tomatoes

1 tablespoon tomato paste

400 g can kidney beans,
   drained and rinsed

400 g cooked skinless chicken
   breast, cut into 2 cm pieces

2 zucchini, cut into 2 cm pieces

1 cup (160 g) frozen corn kernels

⅓ cup (80 g) 99% fat-free plain
   yoghurt

coriander sprigs, to serve

1 Lightly spray a large non-stick frying pan or saucepan
   with oil and heat over medium heat. Cook onion, stirring,
   for 5 minutes or until softened. Add chilli powder and
   cook, stirring, for 1 minute or until fragrant.

2 Add tomatoes, tomato paste and ⅓ cup (80 ml) water
   and bring to the boil. Add kidney beans, chicken, zucchini
   and corn and simmer, stirring, for 5 minutes or until
   chicken is cooked. Sprinkle with black pepper and serve
   with yoghurt and coriander.

Cook's tips

* Store leftovers in an airtight
   container in the fridge for up to
   2 days, or freeze for up to 2 months.

* Add coriander and lime wedges
   to serve. Swap black beans for
   kidney beans if you like.

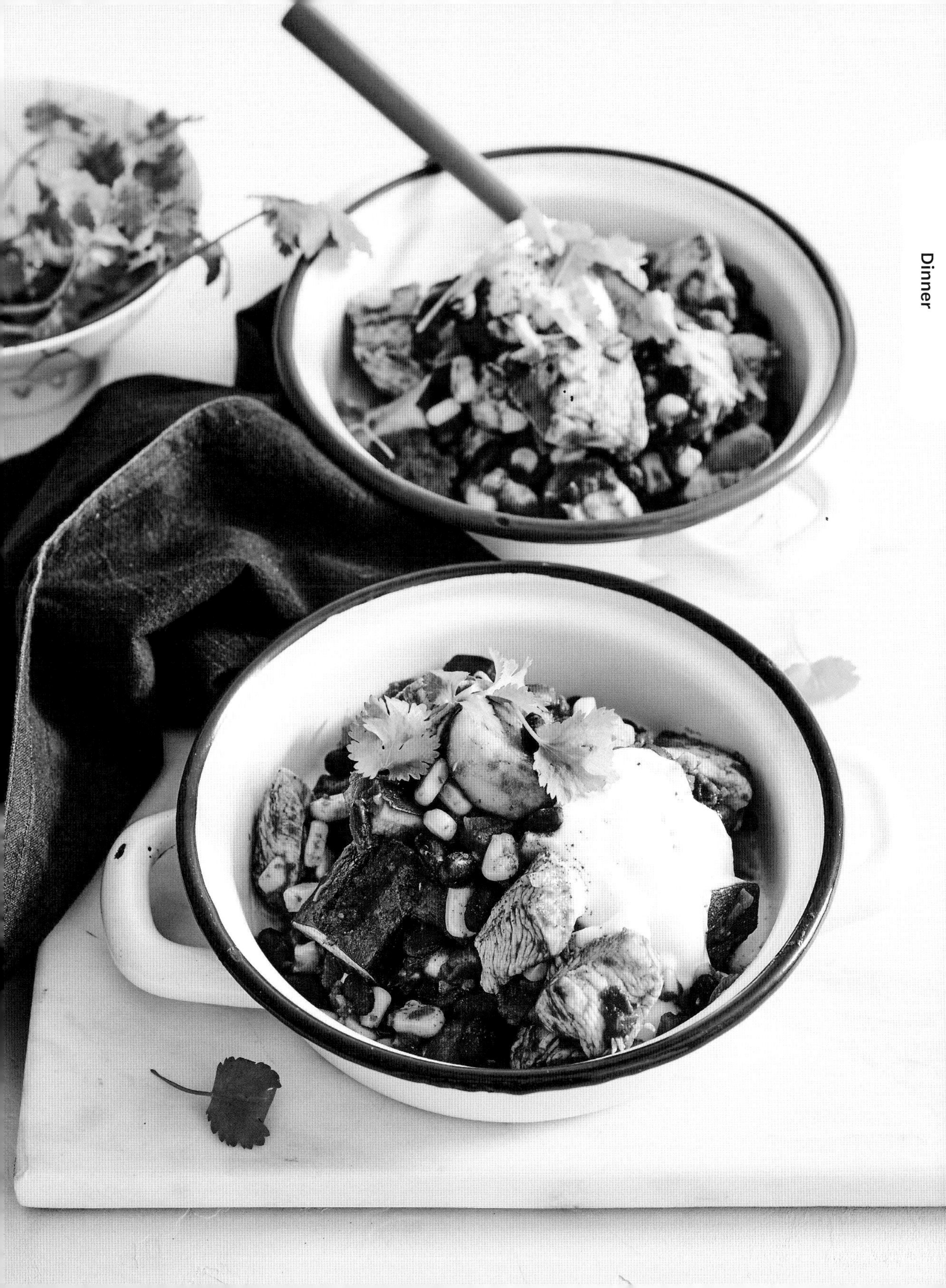

enchiladas

10 **7** **7** SmartPoints value per serve

PREP 20 MIN / **COOK** 30 MIN / **SERVES** 4

300 g skinless chicken
  breast, sliced

1 red onion, thinly sliced

1 red capsicum, thinly sliced

1 garlic clove, crushed

½ teaspoon ground cumin

2 x 125 g cans corn
  kernels, drained

⅔ cup (135 g) canned red kidney
  beans, drained, rinsed and
  gently crushed (see tips)

300 g passata

¼ cup chopped coriander

4 x 40 g wholemeal tortillas

100 ml light sour cream

¼ cup (30 g) grated reduced-fat
  mozzarella

1 Preheat oven to 200°C. Lightly spray an 18 cm x 22 cm rectangular baking dish with oil.

2 Lightly spray a large non-stick frying pan with oil and heat over medium–high heat. Cook chicken, turning, for about 3 minutes or until lightly browned. Add onion and capsicum and cook, stirring, for 4 minutes or until softened. Add garlic and cumin and cook, stirring, for 1 minute or until fragrant. Stir in corn, crushed beans and 200 g passata and bring to the boil. Reduce heat and simmer for 1 minute. Stir in 2 tablespoons coriander.

3 Divide chicken mixture among tortillas and roll up tightly. Place, seam-side down, in prepared dish. Mix remaining passata and sour cream in a jug. Pour evenly over enchiladas and sprinkle with mozzarella. Bake for 15–20 minutes or until golden. Sprinkle with remaining coriander to serve.

Cook's tips

✳ Crush red kidney beans in a small
  bowl using the back of a fork.

✳ For spicy enchiladas, add
  1 teaspoon Mexican chilli powder
  with the garlic and cumin in step 2.

Butter-style *chicken* curry

  SmartPoints value per serve

PREP 15 MIN / **COOK** 50 MIN / **SERVES** 6

2 onions, 1 finely chopped,
   1 finely sliced

2 garlic cloves, crushed

5 cm piece ginger, peeled
   and finely sliced

350 g butternut pumpkin, peeled
   and coarsely chopped

4 cups (1 litre) gluten-free
   vegetable stock (made with
   2 stock cubes)

1⅓ cups (350 g) tomato passata

2 tablespoons mild curry powder

550 g skinless chicken breast,
   cut into 3 cm cubes

1 cup (200 g) white basmati rice

½ teaspoon ground turmeric

200 g baby spinach leaves

½ cup (120 g) 99% fat-free plain
   yoghurt

2 tablespoons chopped coriander

1   Place chopped onion, garlic, ginger, pumpkin and stock in a large saucepan over medium heat. Bring to the boil, then reduce heat and simmer, partially covered, for 12–15 minutes or until vegetables are tender.

2   Strain stock through a sieve set over a large bowl and set aside. Process drained vegetables and passata in a food processor until smooth.

3   Lightly spray a deep frying pan or flameproof casserole dish with oil and heat over medium heat. Cook sliced onion, stirring, for 5–8 minutes or until softened. Add curry powder and cook, stirring, for another 2 minutes. Add chicken and cook, stirring, for 3 minutes, until just sealed, then stir in pureed vegetable mixture and 400 ml reserved stock. Simmer for 20 minutes or until chicken is cooked and sauce has thickened. Season to taste with salt and pepper.

4   Meanwhile, cook rice following packet instructions, adding turmeric to cooking water.

5   When curry is almost cooked, place spinach in a large microwave-safe bowl with 2–3 tablespoons water. Cover and microwave on High (100%) for 2 minutes or until wilted. Drain.

6   Serve curry with turmeric rice, wilted spinach, yoghurt and coriander.

Cook's tip

For a milder curry, reduce curry powder to 1 tablespoon.

The WW Essential Guide to Healthy Eating

Balsamic *and* mustard chicken tray bake

 SmartPoints value per serve

PREP 15 MIN + MARINATING / **COOK** 40 MIN / **SERVES** 4

2 tablespoons balsamic vinegar

1 tablespoon wholegrain mustard

1 tablespoon lemon juice

2 teaspoons olive oil

1 garlic clove, crushed

4 x 180 g skinless chicken breasts

2 carrots, cut into batons

1 red onion, cut into wedges

2 zucchini, cut into batons

2 tablespoons chopped
   flat-leaf parsley

1 Combine vinegar, mustard, lemon juice, oil and garlic in a large snap-lock bag. Season with salt and pepper. Add chicken, seal bag and shake to evenly coat. Place in fridge for 1 hour.

2 Preheat oven to 200°C. Line a large baking tray with baking paper. Spread carrot and onion over prepared tray and lightly spray with oil. Bake for 15 minutes. Place chicken over vegetables and lightly spray with oil. Bake for 15 minutes. Add zucchini and bake for a further 10 minutes or until chicken is cooked through and vegetables are golden and tender. Serve sprinkled with parsley.

Cook's tip

Spice it up by adding a light sprinkling of chilli flakes to serve.

The WW Essential Guide to Healthy Eating

Apricot chicken

 SmartPoints value per serve

PREP 15 MIN / **COOK** 6 HOUR 15 MIN / **SERVES** 4

¼ cup (35 g) plain flour

2 teaspoons smoked paprika

8 x 100 g skinless chicken thigh
fillets, fat trimmed (see tips)

1 tablespoon olive oil

1 onion, chopped

2 garlic cloves, crushed

3 teaspoons korma paste

410 g can apricot halves
in natural juice

½ cup (125 ml) chicken stock

2 tablespoons thyme leaves,
plus extra to serve

1   Combine flour and paprika on a plate. Season with
salt and pepper. Toss chicken in flour mixture to coat.

2   Heat half the oil in a large non-stick frying pan over
medium heat. Cook chicken for 2–3 minutes each side
or until browned. Transfer to a 5.5 litre slow cooker.

3   Heat remaining oil in same pan over medium–high heat.
Cook onion, stirring, for 3–4 minutes or until softened.
Add garlic and curry paste and cook, stirring, for 1 minute
or until fragrant. Add undrained apricots, stock and
thyme and bring to the boil. Season with salt and pepper.

4   Pour mixture over chicken in slow cooker. Cook,
covered, on low for 6 hours (or high for 3 hours).
Serve with extra thyme scattered over the top.

Cook's tips

* If you can't buy small (100 g) thigh
fillets, larger ones will be fine to use,
just ensure you have 800 g in total.

* Serve with steamed asparagus and
baby carrots on the side.

The WW Essential Guide to Healthy Eating

Cheat's lasagne

 SmartPoints value per serve

PREP 15 MIN / **COOK** 30 MIN / **SERVES** 4

1 teaspoon olive oil

1 onion, chopped

3 garlic cloves, crushed

2 carrots, diced

1 zucchini, diced

2 celery sticks, diced

1 tablespoon chopped thyme

300 g extra-lean beef mince

400 g can diced tomatoes

80 g dried lasagne sheets,
   broken into pieces

⅓ cup chopped basil,
   plus extra leaves to serve

⅔ cup (60 g) pizza blend cheese

1   Heat oil in a large deep ovenproof frying pan over high heat. Cook onion, garlic, carrot, zucchini, celery and thyme, stirring, for 10 minutes or until lightly browned. Add mince and cook, stirring to break up any lumps, for 2 minutes or until mince has browned.

2   Stir in tomatoes and 1¼ cups (310 ml) water. Season with salt and pepper and bring to the boil. Push pasta pieces into beef mixture, making sure they are covered. Reduce heat and simmer, covered, stirring occasionally, for 10 minutes. Simmer, uncovered, for a further 5 minutes or until pasta is tender and sauce has thickened.

3   Preheat grill on high. Sprinkle chopped basil and cheese over pasta mixture. Place pan under grill for 2–3 minutes or until cheese is melted and golden. Top with extra basil leaves.

Cook's tip

Serve with mixed baby salad leaves or baby rocket.

Japanese salmon stir-fry

 SmartPoints value per serve

PREP 10 MIN / **COOK** 15 MIN / **SERVES** 4

500 g skinless salmon fillets,
cut into chunks

1½ tablespoons reduced-salt
soy sauce

2 bunches broccolini, cut into
3 cm lengths

1 onion, cut into wedges

1 red capsicum, sliced

2 teaspoons sunflower oil

2 teaspoons sesame oil

1 tablespoon grated ginger

1 tablespoon rice wine vinegar

1 tablespoon mirin seasoning

2 tablespoons sesame seeds,
toasted (see tip)

1   Combine salmon and 2 teaspoons soy sauce in a bowl. Set aside.

2   Heat a wok over high heat. Add broccolini and ¼ cup (60 ml) water. Cook, partially covered, for 3–4 minutes or until water has evaporated and broccolini is bright green and just tender. Transfer to a bowl.

3   Reheat wok over high heat. Add onion, capsicum and ¼ cup (60 ml) water and cook, partially covered, for 3–4 minutes or until water has evaporated and vegetables are just tender. Transfer to bowl with broccolini.

4   Heat half the oils in wok over high heat for 10 seconds. Stir-fry half the salmon for 1–2 minutes or until seared. Transfer to a plate. Repeat with remaining oils and salmon. Return all salmon to wok with ginger and toss to coat. Return vegetables to wok with vinegar, mirin and remaining soy sauce. Stir-fry over high heat until combined and hot. Serve sprinkled with sesame seeds.

Cook's tip

To toast sesame seeds, toss them in a small, dry, non-stick frying pan over medium heat until just golden.

Chicken paella *with* chorizo

  11 SmartPoints value per serve

PREP 15 MIN / **COOK** 40 MIN / **SERVES** 4

100 g chorizo sausage,
   thinly sliced
400 g skinless chicken breasts,
   thinly sliced
1 tablespoon olive oil
1 onion, thinly sliced
1 red capsicum, thinly sliced
3 garlic cloves, crushed
1 teaspoon smoked paprika
200 g white rice
400 g can diced tomatoes
pinch of saffron threads (see tip)
1½ cups (375 ml) chicken stock
½ cup chopped flat-leaf parsley
lemon wedges, to serve

1   Heat a large heavy-based frying pan or paella pan over medium heat. Add chorizo and cook for 1–2 minutes each side or until golden. Transfer to a plate. Add chicken to pan and cook, turning, for 3–4 minutes or until browned. Transfer to a plate.

2   Heat oil in same pan. Add onion, capsicum and garlic and cook, stirring, for 5 minutes or until softened. Add paprika and rice and cook, stirring, for 1 minute.

3   Add tomatoes, saffron and stock and bring to the boil. Return chicken and chorizo to pan and reduce heat to low. Simmer, covered, for 20–25 minutes or until rice is tender. Sprinkle with parsley and serve with lemon wedges.

Cook's tip

Saffron is an expensive spice but a little goes a long way. It's traditionally used in paella and other rice dishes to impart a subtle flavour and a rich golden colour. You'll find it in the herb and spice aisle in supermarkets.

The WW Essential Guide to Healthy Eating

One-pan cauliflower *and* salmon

 SmartPoints value per serve

PREP 5 MIN / **COOK** 15 MIN / **SERVES** 4

1 tablespoon olive oil

650 g cauliflower, cut into florets

1 red onion, cut into wedges

400 g can lentils, drained
   and rinsed

1 teaspoon lemon zest

2 tablespoons lemon juice

300 g hot smoked salmon, flaked

½ cup chopped flat-leaf parsley

lemon wedges, to serve

1   Heat 2 teaspoons olive oil in a large deep frying pan over medium–high heat. Cook cauliflower florets, stirring, for 1 minute. Add ¼ cup (60 ml) water and cook, partially covered, for 3 minutes. Toss and add another ¼ cup (60 ml) water and cook, partially covered, for 4–5 minutes or until cauliflower is just tender and water has evaporated. Transfer to a large bowl.

2   Heat remaining olive oil in same pan over medium–high heat. Cook onion, stirring, for 3 minutes or until golden.

3   Return cauliflower to pan with lentils. Cook over medium heat, stirring, for 1–2 minutes or until hot. Season to taste. Toss through lemon zest and juice, salmon and parsley. Serve with lemon wedges.

Cook's tip

Add ½ teaspoon chilli flakes to pan with onion in step 2 for added flavour and a touch of heat.

The WW Essential Guide to Healthy Eating

Sweet chilli chicken
and cashew stir-fry

 SmartPoints value per serve

PREP 20 MIN / **COOK** 10 MIN / **SERVES** 4

⅓ cup (80 ml) light sweet
   chilli sauce

2 garlic cloves, crushed

1 tablespoon lime juice

1 tablespoon sunflower oil

500 g skinless chicken breast,
   thinly sliced

4 green shallots (spring onions),
   thinly sliced

1 red capsicum, sliced

200 g green beans, trimmed

175 g broccolini, cut into
   5 cm lengths

⅓ cup finely chopped coriander

¼ cup (40 g) unsalted roasted
   cashew nuts, coarsely chopped

1   Combine chilli sauce, garlic and lime juice in a small bowl.
    Set aside.

2   Heat half the oil in a wok over high heat. Stir-fry chicken,
    in batches, for 1–2 minutes or until browned. Transfer to
    a plate.

3   Heat remaining oil in same wok over medium–high
    heat. Add shallot, capsicum, beans, broccolini and 2
    tablespoonss water. Stir-fry for 2–3 minutes or until
    vegetables are tender.

4   Return chicken to wok with reserved sauce mixture
    and stir-fry for 2 minutes or until heated through.
    Serve sprinkled with coriander and cashews.

Cook's tip

**Replace coriander with a handful of
Thai basil leaves, if preferred.**

The WW Essential Guide to Healthy Eating

Creamy chicken *and* mushroom hot pot

④ ② ② **SmartPoints value per serve**

PREP 15 MIN / **COOK** 25 MIN / **SERVES** 4

2 teaspoons olive oil

3 golden shallots, thinly sliced

1 celery stick, thinly sliced

100 g short-cut bacon,
 fat trimmed, chopped

400 g skinless chicken breasts,
 cut into 3 cm pieces

200 g button mushrooms, halved

1 cup (250 ml) salt-reduced
 gluten-free chicken stock

¼ cup (60 ml) reduced-fat
 evaporated milk

1 tablespoon thyme leaves,
 plus extra sprigs to serve

2 teaspoons cornflour

1 Heat oil in a large deep non-stick frying pan over medium–high heat. Cook shallot, celery and bacon, stirring, for 5 minutes or until softened. Add chicken and mushroom and cook, stirring, for 5 minutes or until chicken is browned.

2 Stir in stock, evaporated milk and thyme and bring to a simmer. Simmer, uncovered, for 10 minutes or until chicken is cooked.

3 Combine cornflour and 1 tablespoon water in a small bowl. Add to chicken mixture and stir to combine. Simmer for 2 minutes, stirring, until sauce has thickened. Serve with extra thyme sprigs.

Cook's tip

Serve with steamed green beans and mashed potato. Check your WW app for the additional SmartPoints.

The WW Essential Guide to Healthy Eating

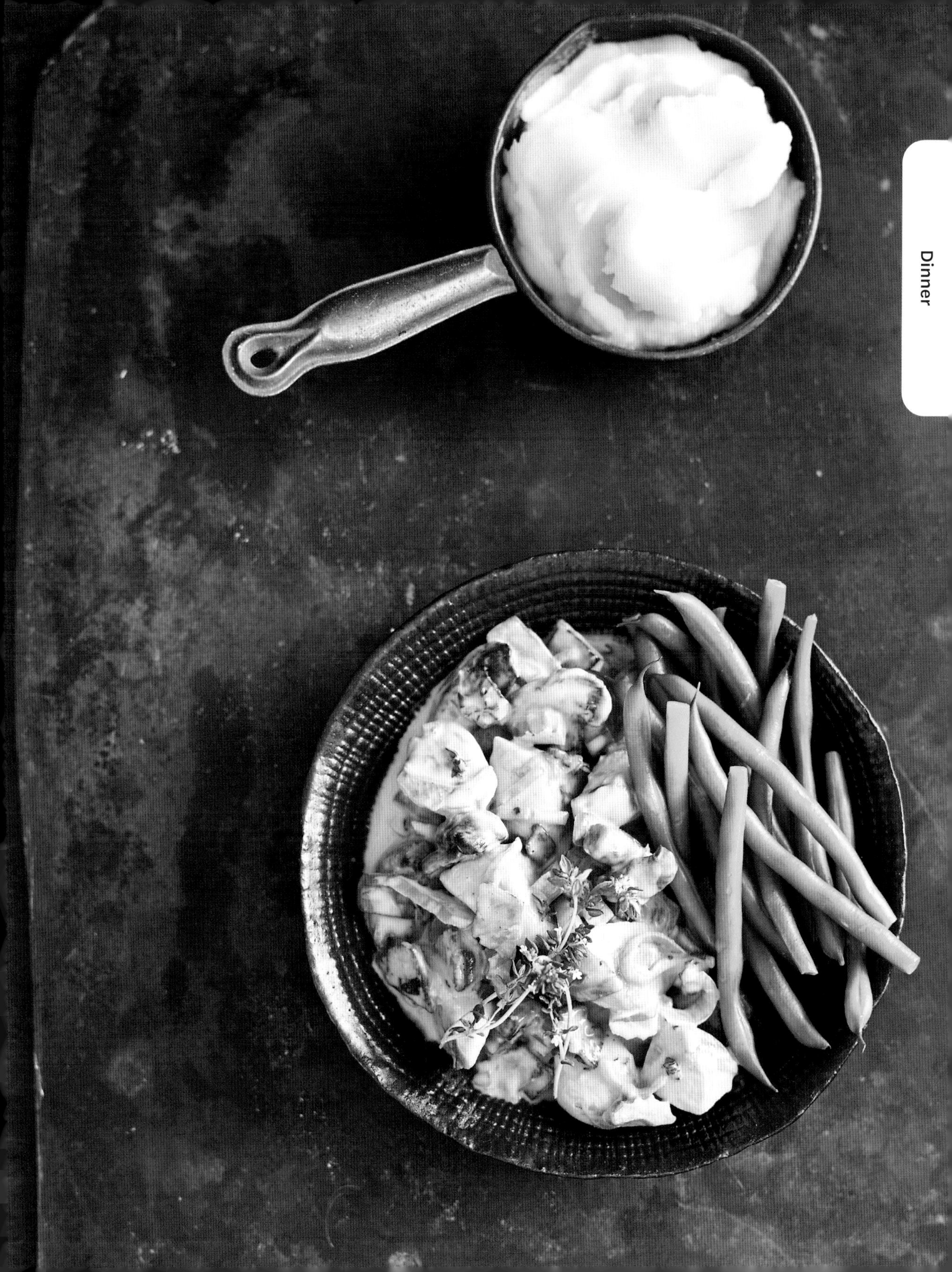

Curried sausage stew

 SmartPoints value per serve

PREP 10 MIN / **COOK** 35 MIN / **SERVES** 4

2 teaspoons olive oil

400 g extra-lean pork sausages

1 onion, coarsely chopped

2 garlic cloves, finely chopped

3 carrots, sliced

3 teaspoons mild curry powder

2 cups (500 ml) beef stock,
    made with 1 gluten-free beef
    stock cube

1 tablespoon tomato chutney

½ cup (60 g) frozen peas

½ cup coriander leaves

1 Heat half the oil in a large deep non-stick frying pan over medium heat. Cook sausages, turning, for 2 minutes or until light golden. Transfer to a plate. Cut in half widthways.

2 Heat remaining oil in same pan over medium heat. Cook onion, garlic and carrot, stirring, for 3 minutes or until softened. Add curry powder and cook, stirring, for 30 seconds or until fragrant. Add stock, chutney and sausages and bring to the boil. Reduce heat and simmer, uncovered, stirring occasionally, for 25 minutes.

3 Add peas and simmer, covered, for 2 minutes or until heated through. Sprinkle with coriander to serve.

Cook's tips

* Replace pork sausages with extra-lean beef sausages, if preferred. Check your WW app for the SmartPoints.

* Serve with steamed green beans.

The WW Essential Guide to Healthy Eating

Pulled lamb tacos
with red cabbage slaw

 SmartPoints value per serve

PREP 20 MIN / **COOK** 8 HOURS 15 MIN / **SERVES** 6

2 teaspoons olive oil

750 g lean boneless easy carve
   lamb shoulder, fat trimmed

2 red onions, finely chopped

3 garlic cloves, crushed

2 teaspoons ground cumin

2 teaspoons sweet paprika

1 tablespoon honey

1 cup (280 g) tomato puree

2 cups (170 g) shredded
   red cabbage

1 carrot, cut into thin matchsticks

2 vine-ripened tomatoes,
   chopped

2 tablespoons chopped coriander

12 x 25 g white corn tortillas
   (see tips)

1   Heat half the oil in a large non-stick frying pan over
    high heat. Cook lamb for 2–3 minutes each side or until
    browned. Transfer to a 5.5 litre slow cooker.

2   Heat remaining oil in same pan over medium heat.
    Cook onion, stirring occasionally, for 5 minutes or until
    softened. Add garlic, cumin and paprika and cook,
    stirring, for 1 minute or until fragrant. Stir in honey,
    tomato puree and ⅓ cup (80 ml) water and bring
    to the boil. Transfer to slow cooker.

3   Cook, covered, on low for 8 hours (or high for 4 hours).
    Remove lamb from cooking liquid. Using two forks,
    coarsely shred lamb and return to sauce.

4   Combine cabbage, carrot, tomato and coriander in
    a large bowl. Top tortillas with pulled lamb and slaw.

Cook's tips

✱ White corn tortillas are gluten free
   and give your tacos an authentic
   Mexican flavour. To heat, follow
   packet instructions.

✱ Serve with baby spinach leaves,
   grilled corn and a dollop of sour
   cream (contains dairy). Check your
   WW app for SmartPoints.

Chicken *with* zucchini cream

  SmartPoints value per serve

PREP 15 MIN / **COOK** 20 MIN / **SERVES** 4

240 g potato, cut into
   5 mm-thick slices

1 red capsicum, thickly sliced

1 green capsicum, thickly sliced

4 x 150 g skinless chicken
   breasts

2 garlic cloves, crushed

1 teaspoon sweet paprika

2 teaspoons olive oil

3 zucchini, coarsely chopped

1 teaspoon lemon zest

1½ tablespoons lemon juice

2 tablespoons tahini

1 Preheat a chargrill or barbecue on medium. Lightly spray potato and capsicums with oil. Cook for 3–5 minutes each side or until lightly charred and tender. Set aside and keep warm (see tip).

2 Meanwhile, combine chicken, half the garlic, paprika and oil in a large bowl. Season with salt and pepper and toss to coat.

3 Reheat chargrill or barbecue on medium–high. Cook chicken for 5 minutes each side or until browned and cooked through. Set aside to rest for 5 minutes. Thickly slice.

4 Meanwhile, place zucchini in a pan of boiling water. Return to the boil, then drain. Process zucchini, lemon zest and juice, tahini and remaining garlic in a food processor until smooth. Transfer to a bowl and season with salt and pepper. Serve chicken with vegetables and zucchini cream.

Cook's tips

* **To keep potato and capsicum warm, place on a baking paper-lined baking tray in a 150°C oven for 10 minutes while cooking chicken.**

* **Serve with baby spinach leaves.**

Vegetarian cottage pie

10 **6** **3** SmartPoints value per serve

PREP 25 MIN / **COOK** 6 HOURS 5 MIN / **SERVES** 4

1 onion, finely chopped

1 carrot, chopped

1 celery stick, chopped

1 cup (200 g) brown lentils,
   drained and rinsed

400 g can diced tomatoes

2 tablespoons herb and garlic
   pizza sauce

1 teaspoon thyme leaves

2 cups (500 ml) vegetable stock

1 tablespoon kecap manis
   (sweet soy sauce)

2 tablespoons chopped
   flat-leaf parsley

680 g potato, chopped

⅓ cup (80 ml) skim milk

2 teaspoons reduced-fat
   oil spread

⅓ cup (40 g) grated vintage
   cheddar cheese

1   Place onion, carrot, celery, lentils, tomatoes, pizza
    sauce, thyme, stock and kecap manis in a 5.5 litre slow
    cooker and stir to combine. Cook, covered, on low for
    6 hours (or high for 3 hours) or until lentils have softened.
    Add parsley and stir to combine. Spoon mixture into
    a 1.5 litre capacity ovenproof dish.

2   Meanwhile, boil, steam or microwave potatoes until
    tender. Drain. Mash in a bowl with milk and spread
    until smooth.

3   Preheat grill on high. Top lentil mixture with mash and
    sprinkle with cheese. Cook for 2–3 minutes or until cheese
    is melted and golden. Serve.

Cook's tips

* You'll find dried lentils in the
  soup aisle of supermarkets.
  Brown lentils can be substituted
  for green lentils, if preferred.

* Serve with a side salad of lettuce
  leaves, halved cherry tomatoes
  and sliced cucumber.

Prawn pad see ew

8 **6** **6** **SmartPoints value per serve**

PREP 15 MIN / **COOK** 10 MIN / **SERVES** 4

2 teaspoons sunflower oil

500 g green prawns,
   peeled and deveined

1 bunch gai lan (Chinese
   broccoli), cut crossways
   into 4 cm pieces

2 garlic cloves, crushed

2 eggs

450 g fresh rice noodles
   (see tips)

⅓ cup (80 ml) kecap manis
   (sweet soy sauce)

2 tablespoons fish sauce

1 long red chilli, thinly sliced,
   to serve

1   Heat half the oil in a large wok over high heat. Stir-fry prawns for 2–3 minutes or until they curl and change colour. Transfer to a plate.

2   Meanwhile, cut any thicker gai lan stems in half lengthways. Add stems to wok and stir-fry for 2 minutes. Add gai lan leaves and garlic and stir-fry for 1 minute or until just tender. Transfer to a plate.

3   Heat remaining oil in the wok. Crack eggs into the centre and stir. Cook for 30 seconds or until the egg is just set. Add noodles, prawns and gai lan and stir-fry for 2 minutes or until heated through. Add kecap manis and fish sauce. Toss to combine. Season with white pepper and serve with chilli.

Cook's tips

* Wok-ready, shelf-fresh rice noodles are available from the noodle aisle in supermarkets. To prepare, follow packet instructions.
* Serve with lemon wedges.

The WW Essential Guide to Healthy Eating

Chilli con carne

8 **5** **5** SmartPoints value per serve

PREP 15 MIN / **COOK** 1 HOUR / **SERVES** 6

1 tablespoon olive oil

500 g lean beef mince

2 onions, finely chopped

1 carrot, diced

2 celery sticks, diced

2 zucchini, diced

1 garlic clove, crushed

2 teaspoons ground cumin

1 teaspoon chilli powder

2 teaspoons ground cinnamon

400 g can diced tomatoes

400 g can red kidney beans,
    drained and rinsed

400 g can chickpeas,
    drained and rinsed

2 tablespoons tomato paste

2 tablespoons balsamic vinegar

⅓ cup coriander leaves, to serve

1   Heat the oil in a large non-stick saucepan over high heat. Cook the mince, breaking up any lumps, for 5 minutes or until browned. Transfer to a large bowl.

2   Lightly spray the saucepan with oil and reduce to medium–high heat. Cook the onion, carrot, celery, zucchini and garlic, stirring, for 8 minutes or until softened. Return the mince to the pan with the cumin, chilli powder and cinnamon. Cook, stirring, for 1 minute or until fragrant. Stir in tomatoes, beans and chickpeas.

3   Whisk 1¾ cups (435 ml) water, tomato paste and balsamic vinegar in a jug until combined. Add to the saucepan and bring to the boil. Reduce heat and simmer, uncovered, stirring occasionally, for 45 minutes or until thickened.

4   Top with coriander to serve.

Cook's tip

Serve with ½ cup (85 g) steamed rice (per serve). Check your WW app for SmartPoints. For a ZeroPoints side, serve with fresh or lightly steamed baby spinach.

Sicilian *chicken* casserole

 SmartPoints value per serve

PREP 15 MIN / **COOK** 45 MIN / **SERVES** 4

2 teaspoons olive oil

4 x 150 g skinless chicken thigh
fillets, fat trimmed

1 red onion, thinly sliced

2 celery sticks, sliced

2 garlic cloves, crushed

1 tablespoon chopped oregano,
plus extra leaves to serve

400 g cherry tomatoes

1 tablespoon baby capers,
rinsed and drained

½ teaspoon chilli flakes
(optional)

400 g can cannellini beans,
drained and rinsed

1   Preheat oven to 180°C. Lightly spray a 1.25-litre capacity
ovenproof dish with oil.

2   Heat 1 teaspoon oil in a large non-stick frying pan over
medium–high heat. Cook chicken for 1–2 minutes each
side or until golden. Place in prepared dish.

3   Return pan to medium heat. Add remaining oil, onion and
celery and cook, stirring, for 5 minutes or until softened.
Add garlic and oregano and cook, stirring, for 1 minute
or until fragrant. Add tomatoes, capers, chilli flakes
(if using) and ¼ cup (60 ml) water and bring to the boil.
Reduce heat and simmer, uncovered, for 5 minutes. Stir
in cannellini beans. Season with salt and pepper. Pour
tomato mixture over chicken.

4   Cover with foil and bake for 30 minutes or until chicken
is very tender. Remove foil for last 10 minutes of cooking
time. Serve sprinkled with extra oregano leaves and
seasoned with pepper.

Serve with steamed green beans.

Slow-cooked chicken *with* risoni, feta *and* oregano

 SmartPoints value per serve

PREP 25 MIN / **COOK** 6 HOURS 15 MIN / **SERVES** 4

1 tablespoon olive oil

8 x 100 g skinless chicken lovely
   leg pieces

1 red onion, thinly sliced

1 carrot, chopped

2 celery sticks, chopped

3 garlic cloves, thinly sliced

1 teaspoon dried oregano

¼ cup (60 ml) dry white wine

2 dried bay leaves

400 g can diced tomatoes

1½ cups (375 ml) salt-reduced
   chicken stock

⅓ cup (75 g) risoni

50 g reduced-fat feta, crumbled

2 tablespoons oregano leaves

1   Heat half the oil in a large non-stick frying pan over high heat. Cook chicken, turning, for 5 minutes or until browned. Transfer to a 5.5 litre slow cooker.

2   Heat remaining oil in same pan over medium heat. Add onion, carrot and celery and cook, stirring occasionally, for 5 minutes or until softened. Add garlic and dried oregano and cook for 1 minute or until fragrant. Stir in wine, bay leaves, tomatoes and stock and bring to the boil. Transfer to slow cooker.

3   Cook, covered, on low for 5 hours (or high for 2½ hours). Stir in risoni. Cook, covered, on low for 1 hour (or high for 30 minutes) or until risoni is tender and chicken is cooked through. Serve topped with feta and oregano.

Cook's tips

* Serve with steamed beans and zucchini slices.

* Chicken lovely legs are chicken legs with the skin and some of the bone removed. Find them in the meat cabinets at most supermarkets or specialty chicken stores.

Spinach *and* ricotta cannelloni

  SmartPoints value per serve

PREP 20 MIN / **COOK** 30 MIN + STANDING / **SERVES** 4

500 g frozen spinach,
   thawed, drained

300 g reduced-fat ricotta

250 g dried cannelloni tubes

700 g tomato passata

½ cup (60 g) coarsely grated
   reduced-fat tasty cheese

1   Preheat oven to 180°C. Lightly spray a 2-litre capacity, ovenproof dish with oil.

2   Squeeze spinach with hands to remove excess water. Place in a bowl with ricotta and season with salt and pepper. Stir to combine.

3   Spoon ricotta mixture into each cannelloni tube. Spread half the passata over base of prepared dish. Arrange cannelloni, side-by-side, over passata. Pour remaining passata over pasta. Sprinkle with cheese. Bake for 30 minutes or until pasta is tender and filling is heated through. Cover with foil and set aside for 10 minutes to stand before serving.

Cook's tips

* Recipe can be prepared several hours ahead. Keep covered in the fridge. To cook, uncover dish and transfer to preheated oven, adding an extra 5 minutes cooking time.

* Traditional cannelloni recipes can be up to 17 SmartPoints per serve. WW's version of the classic is healthier by using reduced-fat cheese and passata.

Chicken dumplings *in* Asian broth

 SmartPoints value per serve

PREP 25 MIN / **COOK** 20 MIN / **SERVES** 4

200 g chicken breast mince

1 garlic clove, crushed

1 teaspoon grated ginger

50 g canned water chestnuts,
   drained, rinsed and finely
   chopped

1 long red chilli, finely chopped

2 green shallots (spring onions),
   thinly sliced

¼ cup (60 ml) soy sauce

20 wonton wrappers

BROTH

4 cups (1 litre) chicken stock

1 garlic clove, thinly sliced

2 cm piece ginger,
   thinly sliced

2 tablespoons fish sauce

2 tablespoons lime juice

1 bunch choy sum,
   coarsely chopped

2 cups (70 g) bean sprouts

½ cup coriander leaves

1   Combine chicken mince, garlic, ginger, water chestnuts, half the chilli, half the shallot and 2 teaspoons soy sauce in a bowl. Arrange wonton wrappers on a workbench. Place a heaped teaspoon of mince mixture in the centre of each wonton wrapper and brush edges with a little water. Gather edges around filling to enclose and pinch together to seal.

2   To make broth, bring stock, sliced garlic and ginger, fish sauce, lime juice, remaining soy sauce and 2 cups (500 ml) water to the boil in a large saucepan. Reduce heat to low and simmer, covered, for 10 minutes. Using a slotted spoon, remove and discard garlic and ginger.

3   Add wontons to broth and simmer for 2 minutes, then add choy sum and cook for 2–3 minutes or until wontons are cooked through and choy sum is just tender.

4   Using a slotted spoon, transfer chicken dumplings and choy sum into serving bowls. Ladle broth into bowls and serve topped with bean sprouts, coriander leaves and remaining chopped chilli and julienned shallot.

Cook's tip

Wonton filling can be made several hours ahead. Keep covered in the fridge.

Classic beef stew

 SmartPoints value per serve

PREP 25 MIN / **COOK** 2 HOURS 20 MIN / **SERVES** 4

1 tablespoon olive oil

600 g lean beef chuck steak, fat
   trimmed, cut into 3 cm pieces

1 onion, chopped

1 tablespoon plain flour

400 g can diced tomatoes

¾ cup (185 ml) beef stock

300 g potato, cut into
   3 cm pieces

2 carrots, sliced

1 swede, chopped

200 g button mushrooms,
   halved

3 cups (60 g) baby
   spinach leaves

1   Heat oil in a large deep non-stick saucepan over medium–high heat. Cook beef, in batches, turning, for 3 minutes or until browned. Transfer to a plate.

2   Reduce heat to medium. Cook onion in same pan, stirring, for 5 minutes or until softened. Add flour and cook, stirring, for 1 minute. Stir in tomatoes, stock and beef and bring to the boil. Reduce heat and simmer, covered, stirring occasionally, for 1 hour (see tip).

3   Add potato, carrot, swede and mushroom. Simmer, covered, stirring occasionally, for 1 hour or until beef is very tender. Add spinach and cook for 1 minute or until just wilted. Serve.

Cook's tips

* **Stir beef occasionally to stop it catching and burning on the bottom of the pan.**

* **Store any leftovers in an airtight container in the fridge for up to 2 days, or freeze for up to 3 months. Reheat in the microwave or in a saucepan on the stovetop.**

Shepherd's pie *with* celeriac

7 **7** **6** SmartPoints value per serve

PREP 15 MIN / **COOK** 50 MIN / **SERVES** 6

450 g potato, chopped

600 g celeriac, chopped

¼ cup (60 ml) skim milk

2 teaspoons olive oil

2 onions, finely chopped

2 carrots, diced

1 zucchini, diced

3 garlic cloves, crushed

750 g lean lamb mince

2 teaspoons cornflour

⅓ cup (90 g) tomato paste

1 tablespoon gluten-free
   Worcestershire sauce

1 cup (250 ml) beef stock

3⅓ cups (65 g) baby
   spinach leaves

2 tomatoes, sliced

1 Cook potato and celeriac in a large saucepan of salted boiling water for 20 minutes or until tender. Drain and return to pan. Heat over low heat for 1 minute to dry out. Add milk and mash well. Season with salt and pepper.

2 Meanwhile, preheat oven to 200°C. Heat oil in a large frying pan over medium heat. Cook onion, carrot, zucchini and garlic, stirring, for 10 minutes or until softened. Add mince and cook over high heat, stirring to break up any lumps, for 5 minutes or until browned.

3 Whisk cornflour, tomato paste, Worcestershire sauce and beef stock in a jug until smooth. Add to lamb mixture and bring to the boil. Reduce heat and simmer for 5 minutes or until thickened slightly. Stir through spinach. Spoon into a 19 cm x 29 cm 2-litre capacity ovenproof dish. Top with tomato slices and spread over mashed potato. Use a fork to create small peaks in the mash. Place dish on a baking tray and bake for 30 minutes or until top is golden.

Cook's tip

Serve with a salad of mixed leaves, seasoned with salt and pepper and drizzled with balsamic vinegar.

Zoodle bolognese

PREP 10 MIN / **COOK** 25 MIN / **SERVES** 4

500 g extra-lean beef mince

1 onion, finely chopped

1 garlic clove, crushed

400 g can diced tomatoes

450 g tomato passata

1½ tablespoons tomato paste

1 teaspoon dried mixed herbs

1 gluten-free beef stock cube

3 zucchini, spiralised (see tip)

small basil leaves, to serve

1   Lightly spray a large non-stick saucepan with oil and heat over medium heat. Add mince, onion and garlic and cook, breaking up any lumps, for 5 minutes or until mince is browned and onion is softened.

2   Add tomatoes, passata, tomato paste and mixed herbs to pan, stir well and bring to the boil. Crumble in stock cube and stir again. Reduce heat and simmer, stirring occasionally, for 15–20 minutes or until sauce has thickened.

3   When sauce is nearly ready, lightly spray a large frying pan with oil and heat over medium heat. Add zucchini and cook, stirring, for 1–2 minutes or until slightly softened. Season to taste, divide among plates and top with sauce. Garnish with basil.

Cook's tip

The WW Triple Blade Spiraliser makes spiralising zucchini easy. The handy kitchen tool, which also spiralises a variety of fruits and vegetables, is available from the WW Shop (ww.com/shop).

Thai *yellow* fish curry

 SmartPoints value per serve

PREP 10 MIN / COOK 10 MIN / SERVES 4

1 red onion, thickly sliced

3 cm piece ginger, shredded

2 tablespoons yellow
  curry paste

1 cup (250 ml) light
  coconut milk

1 cup (250 ml) fish stock

115 g baby corn, halved
  lengthways

1 red capsicum, sliced

500 g skinless firm white fish
  fillets, cut into 3 cm pieces

150 g snow peas, halved

1 cup Thai basil leaves

1. Heat a non-stick wok over medium–high heat. Stir-fry onion and ginger for 2–3 minutes or until just tender. Add curry paste and stir-fry for 1 minute or until fragrant.

2. Add coconut milk, stock, corn, capsicum and fish. Reduce heat and simmer, covered, for 4–5 minutes or until fish is cooked. Stir in snow peas and half the basil. Sprinkle with remaining basil to serve.

Cook's tip

Serve with ½ cup (85 g) steamed brown rice per serve. Check your WW app for additional SmartPoints.

The WW Essential Guide to Healthy Eating

BBQ chicken *and* bacon pizza

 9 8 8 SmartPoints value per serve

PREP 10 MIN / **COOK** 20 MIN / **SERVES** 4

60 g short-cut bacon,
fat trimmed, sliced

2 x 100 g wholemeal Lebanese
breads

½ cup (130 g) tomato passata

150 g button mushrooms,
thinly sliced

½ red capsicum, thinly sliced

½ red onion, thinly sliced

200 g cooked skinless chicken
breast, shredded

1 cup (120 g) shredded
reduced-fat mozzarella

2 tablespoons barbecue sauce

1   Preheat oven to 200°C. Line two baking trays with baking paper.

2   Heat a small non-stick frying pan over medium heat. Cook bacon, stirring, for 3–4 minutes or until just browned.

3   Place Lebanese bread on prepared trays. Spread passata over bread. Top with mushroom, capsicum, onion, chicken and bacon. Season with pepper. Sprinkle with mozzarella and drizzle with barbecue sauce. Bake for 15 minutes or until bases become crisp and golden.

Cook's tips

* Serve with a salad of lettuce, thinly sliced red onion and baby roma tomatoes, drizzled with balsamic vinegar.

* Cover and refrigerate any leftover pizza and serve cold or warmed for lunch the next day.

Slow-cooker *Moroccan* lamb *and* chickpea soup

 SmartPoints value per serve

PREP 10 MIN / **COOK** 8 HOURS 10 MIN / **SERVES** 4

2 x 250 g lean lamb shanks,
    fat trimmed

1 onion, finely chopped

2 celery sticks, sliced

2 carrots, sliced

1½ tablespoons Moroccan
    seasoning

4 tomatoes, finely chopped

4 cups (1 litre) reduced-salt
    beef stock

2 x 400 g can chickpeas,
    drained and rinsed

2 cups (60 g) finely shredded
    curly kale

½ cup flat-leaf parsley leaves

1   Heat a large non-stick frying pan over high heat.
    Cook shanks, turning, for 5 minutes or until browned.
    Transfer to a 5.5-litre capacity slow cooker.

2   Reheat same frying pan over medium–high heat. Cook
    onion, celery and carrot, stirring, for 5 minutes or until
    vegetables have softened. Add Moroccan seasoning and
    cook, stirring, for 30 seconds or until fragrant. Transfer to
    slow cooker.

3   Add tomato and stock to slow cooker. Cook, covered, on
    low for 8 hours (or high for 4 hours) or until meat is very
    tender and falling off the bone. Remove shanks and set
    aside for 10 minutes or until cool enough to handle. Using
    two forks, shred lamb meat. Discard fat and bones.

4   Meanwhile, add chickpeas and kale to slow cooker and
    cook, covered, on high for 15 minutes or until kale has
    wilted. Stir through shredded lamb and serve topped
    with parsley.

Cook's tip

To cook this on the stovetop, use a
heavy-based saucepan and simmer,
covered, for 1½–2 hours or until meat
is falling off the bone. Add more
liquid if it is evaporating too much.
Add kale and chickpeas for the last
5 minutes of cooking.

The WW Essential Guide to Healthy Eating

Chicken parmigiana

(8) (6) (6) **SmartPoints value per serve**

PREP 20 MIN / **COOK** 40 MIN / **SERVES** 6

1 tablespoon olive oil

1 garlic clove, crushed

¼ cup basil leaves, sliced

2 cups (520 g) tomato passata

1 egg

¼ cup (60 ml) milk

150 g breadcrumbs

¼ cup finely chopped chives

2 x 375 g skinless
chicken breasts

⅓ cup (50 g) plain flour

120 g lean leg ham

½ cup (60 g) reduced-fat
grated mozzarella

1   Preheat oven to 160°C. Heat half the oil in a small saucepan over medium heat. Add garlic and basil and cook, stirring, for 30 seconds or until fragrant. Add passata and bring to the boil. Reduce heat to low and simmer, uncovered, for 6–8 minutes or until thickened. Set aside.

2   Whisk egg and milk in a shallow bowl. Combine breadcrumbs and chives on a plate. Cut chicken breasts in half horizontally. Pound each piece to 4 mm thick with a meat mallet between two pieces of baking paper. Toss chicken in flour, shaking off excess. Dip chicken, one piece at a time, in egg mixture, then coat in breadcrumb mixture.

3   Heat remaining oil in a large non-stick frying pan over medium–high heat. Add chicken and cook for 2–3 minutes each side or until lightly browned. Line a baking tray with baking paper and lightly spray with oil. Place chicken on prepared tray.

4   Top chicken with tomato mixture, then ham and mozzarella. Bake for 20 minutes or until cheese melts and chicken is cooked through. Serve with basil leaves scattered over the top.

Cook's tip

**Serve with baby rocket leaves
or mixed salad leaves.**

Garlic prawns *with* chilli

 SmartPoints value per serve

PREP 20 MIN / **COOK** 10 MIN / **SERVES** 4

500 g peeled green prawns,
  deveined (see tips)
1 tablespoon olive oil
1 tablespoon reduced-fat
  oil spread
3 garlic cloves, crushed
1 long red chilli, finely chopped
¼ cup finely chopped
  flat-leaf parsley
lemon wedges, to serve

1 Using a sharp knife, make a cut along the belly of each prawn (being careful not to cut all the way through). Open out and press lightly to flatten.

2 Heat a large non-stick frying pan over medium heat. Add oil and spread and heat for 30 seconds or until spread has melted. Add garlic and chilli and cook, stirring, for 30 seconds or until fragrant.

3 Increase heat to medium–high. Add prawns and cook, stirring, for 5 minutes or until just cooked through. Stir in parsley. Serve with lemon wedges.

Cook's tips

* To devein prawns, grab the vein from the head of the prawn with your fingers and carefully pull it out.

* Serve with whole grain sourdough bread (contains gluten), if desired. Check your WW app for SmartPoints.

Dessert

Mango *and* vanilla ice-cream terrine

 SmartPoints value per serve

PREP 45 MIN / **COOK** 10 MIN + OVERNIGHT FREEZING / **SERVES** 10

650 g reduced-fat vanilla
  ice-cream

⅓ cup (75 g) caster sugar

1½ tablespoons lime juice

3 mangoes

1 egg white, lightly beaten

7 x 12 g sponge finger biscuits

2 tablespoons fresh
  passionfruit pulp

1   Lightly spray a 7 cm-deep, 9 cm x 25.5 cm (base measurement) loaf tin with oil. Line base and sides with baking paper, allowing 5 cm to hang over both long sides. Spread half the ice-cream over base of prepared tin. Cover with plastic wrap and freeze until required.

2   Combine sugar and ⅓ cup (80 ml) water in a small saucepan over medium heat. Cook, stirring, for 4–5 minutes or until sugar has dissolved. Bring to the boil. Reduce heat and simmer, uncovered, for 5 minutes or until slightly thickened. Cool. Stir in lime juice.

3   Chop flesh of 2 mangoes. Place in a food processor or blender and process until smooth. Add sugar syrup and process until combined. Pour into a freezer-proof container. Cover with plastic wrap and freeze for 3 hours or until firm. Remove mango mixture from container and use a knife to coarsely chop. Place in a food processor with egg white and process until combined and smooth. Spread over vanilla ice-cream in tin. Smooth top and freeze for 3 hours or until firm.

4   Spread remaining ice-cream evenly over mango layer in tin. Lightly press biscuits into ice-cream. Cover and freeze overnight or until firm. Invert terrine onto a serving platter. Thinly slice remaining mango. Top terrine with mango and passionfruit pulp. Cut into slices to serve.

Cook's tip

For a raspberry and vanilla ice-cream terrine, swap lime juice with lemon juice, 2 mangoes with 400 g frozen raspberries, and sliced mango and passionfruit with 125 g strawberries (quartered) and 60 g each of raspberries and blueberries.

Affogato

5 **5** **5** **SmartPoints value per serve**

PREP 5 MIN / **SERVES** 2

1 tablespoon instant coffee
   granules

2 x 80 g scoops reduced-fat
   vanilla ice-cream

2 tablespoons marsala wine
   (see tip)

20 g almond bread (see tip)

1 Combine coffee with ½ cup (125 ml) boiling water in
   a heatproof jug. Stir until dissolved.

2 Place ice-cream into two heatproof serving glasses.
   Pour over the marsala and hot coffee. Serve immediately
   with almond bread.

Cook's tips

✳ You can use Kahlua, Tia Maria
   or Frangelico liqueurs instead
   of marsala.

✳ Similar to Italian biscotti, almond
   bread is a sweet bread, cut into
   wafer-thin slices and baked
   until crisp. It's available from
   continental delicatessens and
   major supermarkets.

Easy chocolate brownies

 4 **3** **3** **SmartPoints value per serve**

PREP 10 MIN / **COOK** 20 MIN / **SERVES** 16

1 cup (90 g) cocoa powder

½ teaspoon baking powder

150 g caster sugar

200 g 99% fat-free plain yoghurt

1 egg, lightly beaten

2 teaspoons vanilla extract

25 g dark chocolate chips

1   Preheat oven to 190°C. Lightly spray a 20 cm square cake tin with oil and line base with baking paper.

2   Sift cocoa powder, baking powder and ¼ teaspoon salt into a large mixing bowl. Add sugar and stir to combine. Stir in yoghurt, egg, vanilla and chocolate until combined.

3   Spoon mixture into prepared tin and level top. Bake for 20 minutes or until almost set. Cool in tin for 15 minutes before turning out onto a board. Cut into 16 squares.

Cook's tip

Leftover brownies will keep in an airtight container in the fridge for up to 5 days. Warm individual brownies in microwave on High (100%) for 20 seconds.

The WW Essential Guide to Healthy Eating

Instant strawberry ice-cream

 SmartPoints value per serve

PREP 5 MIN / **SERVES** 4

2 chopped frozen bananas

500 g packet frozen sliced
    strawberries

¼ cup (20 g) rolled oats

¼ cup (60 g) 99% fat-free
    plain yoghurt

1 teaspoon rosewater

1   Process banana, strawberries, oats, yoghurt and
rosewater in a food processor, stopping to scrape down
the side occasionally, until a thick paste forms. Scoop
into serving bowls. Serve immediately.

Cook's tips

* You can use any frozen berries,
such as raspberries or blackberries,
instead of strawberries. The
SmartPoints values remain
the same.

* Store any leftovers in a freezer-proof
container, with plastic wrap on the
surface, for up to 1 month. Allow to
soften slightly before serving.

Cinnamon *and* pear tea cake

4 **4** **4** SmartPoints value per serve

PREP 20 MIN / **COOK** 30 MIN / **SERVES** 8

75 g reduced-fat oil spread

⅓ cup (75 g) granulated stevia

1 egg

2 teaspoons vanilla extract

½ teaspoon ground cinnamon

1 cup (150 g) self-raising
    flour, sifted

⅓ cup (80 ml) skim milk

1 pear, thinly sliced (see tip)

1   Preheat oven to 160°C. Lightly spray a 20 cm round springform tin with oil. Line base with baking paper. Reserve 2 teaspoons spread and 2 teaspoons stevia.

2   Using electric beaters, beat remaining spread and stevia with egg, vanilla extract and half the cinnamon in a bowl until combined. Stir in half the flour, then milk. Stir in remaining flour until combined. Spoon mixture into prepared tin. Using a spatula, smooth the surface. Arrange pear slices on top in a circular pattern.

3   Bake for 30 minutes or until a skewer inserted in the centre comes out clean. Set cake aside in tin to cool for 5 minutes, then remove side of tin and transfer cake to a wire rack.

4   Place reserved spread in a small microwave-safe dish. Microwave on High (100%) for 5–10 seconds or until melted. Combine remaining cinnamon and reserved stevia in a small bowl. Brush hot cake with melted spread. Sprinkle with cinnamon mixture. Serve warm or at room temperature.

Cook's tips

* **Any type of pear is suitable. You can also use apple instead of pear.**

* **Store cooled leftovers in an airtight container for up to 3 days.**

cheesecake

5 **5** **5** SmartPoints value per serve

PREP 15 MIN + 3 HRS CHILLING / **COOK** 5 MIN / **SERVES** 12

160 g sponge finger biscuits

3 teaspoons powdered gelatine

250 g light cream cheese

250 g ricotta

2 teaspoons lemon zest

⅓ cup (75 g) granulated stevia

2 tablespoons lemon juice

170 g 99% fat-free
   plain yoghurt

1 lemon, thinly sliced

1   Line base and side of a 22 cm round springform cake tin with baking paper. Arrange sponge fingers over base of prepared tin, trimming to fit. Discard trimmings.

2   Sprinkle gelatine over 2 tablespoons boiling water in a small heatproof jug. Stir with a fork until gelatine dissolves. Be careful not to stir for too long; if mixture becomes thick and opaque you have overworked the gelatine.

3   Using electric beaters, beat cheeses, zest and half the stevia in a bowl until smooth. Beat in gelatine mixture. Beat in lemon juice and yoghurt.

4   Pour mixture over sponge fingers and smooth surface. Refrigerate for 3 hours or until set.

5   Place lemon slices, remaining stevia and 2 tablespoons water in a small saucepan over medium heat. Stir until stevia dissolves. Bring to the boil. Gently boil for 3–4 minutes or until syrup thickens and lemon turns slightly golden. Cool.

6   Remove cheesecake from tin, discard baking paper. Transfer to a serving plate. Serve topped with candied lemon and drizzled with syrup.

The WW Essential Guide to Healthy Eating

Sarah's apple berry crumble slice

3 **3** **1** SmartPoints value per serve

PREP 15 MIN / **COOK** 30 MIN / **SERVES** 16

100 g medjool dates, pitted
   and chopped

1¾ cups (155 g) rolled oats

½ cup (40 g) desiccated coconut

1 egg

2 tablespoons plain flour,
   plus 1 teaspoon extra

1 tablespoon brown sugar

1½ tablespoons reduced-fat
   oil spread

400 g can apple slices
   (see tip)

½ cup (60 g) frozen raspberries

1 Preheat oven to 180°C. Lightly spray a 19 cm (base measurement) square cake tin with oil. Line base and sides with baking paper, allowing paper to extend 3 cm over edges of tin.

2 Place dates and 1 tablespoon water in a microwave-safe dish. Cover and microwave on High (100%) for 1 minute or until soft.

3 Process 1½ cups oats, ¼ cup coconut, egg and dates in a food processor until well combined and mixture comes together. Press mixture into base of prepared tin. Bake for 10–12 minutes or until golden.

4 Meanwhile, to make crumble, combine remaining oats and coconut with flour and sugar in a bowl. Using your fingertips, rub in spread until mixture resembles coarse breadcrumbs.

5 Combine apple, raspberries and extra flour in a bowl. Spoon apple mixture over base and sprinkle with crumble mixture. Bake for 15 minutes or until crumble is golden. Set aside to cool for 10 minutes before removing from tin and cutting into squares. Serve warm.

Cook's tips

* Apple slices are available in the canned fruit section of supermarkets.
* This slice is best eaten on the day it is made. Add 99% fat-free plain yoghurt to serve. Check your WW app for the SmartPoints.
* You can swap raspberries for blackberries.

Member recipe
by Sarah Van Dyke
Find more of Sarah's recipes
@sarahs_recipes

Chocolate self-saucing pudding

 5 **5** **5** SmartPoints value per serve

PREP 10 MIN / **COOK** 35 MIN / **SERVES** 6

1 cup (150 g) self-raising flour
¼ cup (25 g) dark cocoa powder
½ cup (110 g) granulated stevia
½ cup (125 ml) skim milk
1 egg
50 g reduced-fat oil spread,
    melted, cooled
1 teaspoon vanilla extract

1 Preheat oven to 180°C. Lightly spray a 4-cup (1 litre) capacity baking dish with oil.

2 Sift flour and 1 tablespoon of cocoa powder into a bowl. Stir in half the stevia and make a well in centre.

3 Use a fork to whisk milk, egg, spread and vanilla in a jug.

4 Pour wet mixture over dry ingredients and fold until just combined. Spread evenly into prepared dish.

5 Reserve 1 teaspoon of remaining cocoa powder and sift remaining over surface of batter. Sprinkle with remaining stevia. Carefully pour 1½ cups (375 ml) boiling water over batter (over back of a spoon to prevent holes). Bake for 30–35 minutes or until firm to a gentle touch. Sprinkle with reserved cocoa powder and serve warm.

Cook's tip

Serve with 99% fat-free Greek-style yoghurt. Check your WW app for the SmartPoints.

Apple pie

7 **6** **6** SmartPoints value per serve

PREP 30 MIN / **COOK** 50 MIN / **SERVES** 6

1 kg apples, quartered, cored
    and cut into 1 cm-thick slices
2 tablespoons brown sugar
1 tablespoon lemon juice
1 tablespoon cornflour
1 x 170 g sheet frozen reduced-
    fat puff pastry, just thawed
¾ cup (110 g) plain flour
1 tablespoon icing sugar
¼ teaspoon bicarbonate of soda
⅓ cup (80 g) 99% fat-free
    plain yoghurt
1½ tablespoon skim milk
2 teaspoons raw sugar

1   Preheat oven to 200°C. Combine apple, brown sugar and lemon juice in a saucepan over medium heat. Cook, covered, for 10 minutes or until apple is tender but still holds its shape. Remove from heat, sprinkle cornflour over apple and stir until well combined. Transfer mixture to a large bowl. Set aside to cool.

2   Meanwhile, place pastry on a baking paper-lined baking tray. Lightly spray a 24 cm (top measurement) pie tin with oil. Invert pie tin over pastry and run a small knife the around edge to cut out 24 cm round. Discard trimmings. Cut out small leaf shapes from pastry round and place on same tray. Refrigerate.

3   Sift flour, icing sugar, bicarbonate of soda and ¼ teaspoon salt into a bowl. Whisk yoghurt and 1 tablespoon milk in a small bowl until combined. Stir yoghurt mixture into flour mixture until combined. Knead dough on a lightly floured surface until smooth. Roll out on floured surface to make a 28 cm round. Line prepared tin with pastry, allowing it to hang over the edge. Fill with apple mixture.

4   Cover filling with puff pastry round, pressing the edge to seal. Trim edges, then decorate pie top with pastry leaves. Brush with remaining milk and sprinkle with raw sugar. Bake for 40–45 minutes or until the pastry is golden and puffed. Serve pie warm or at room temperature.

Nutty ice-cream waffle cones

 8 8 8 SmartPoints value per serve

PREP 10 MIN + 3–4 HRS FREEZING / **SERVES** 8

480 g reduced-fat vanilla
    ice-cream, softened
½ cup (95 g) red sugar-coated
    (Vienna) almonds, coarsely
    chopped, plus 2 tablespoons
    extra (see tip)
8 x 14 g waffle cones

1   Place ice-cream in a large bowl. Add almonds, stirring until well combined. Transfer to an airtight container, cover and place in freezer for 3–4 hours or until firm.

2   Scoop ice-cream into waffle cones and serve sprinkled with extra almonds. Serve immediately.

Cook's tips

✱ **Also known as French vanilla almonds, Vienna almonds are sugar coated. They are available from delicatessens and specialty nut stores. If you cannot find Vienna almonds, sub in regular almonds.**

✱ **You can use plain cones instead of waffle cones or serve in bowls.**

The WW Essential Guide to Healthy Eating

Baked *custard* tarts

6 **6** **6** SmartPoints value per serve

PREP 30 MIN / **COOK** 30 MIN + COOLING / **SERVES** 12

1 egg

2 egg yolks

½ cup (110 g) caster sugar

2 tablespoons cornflour

1 teaspoon vanilla extract

1⅔ cups (415 ml) skim milk

2 x 200 g frozen reduced-fat
   shortcrust pastry sheets,
   thawed

¼ teaspoon ground nutmeg

1   Whisk egg, yolks, sugar, cornflour and vanilla extract
    in a bowl until combined. Bring milk just to the boil in
    a saucepan over medium heat. Gradually whisk milk
    into egg mixture until combined. Pour mixture back
    into saucepan over medium heat. Cook, stirring, for
    3–5 minutes or until mixture boils and thickens. Transfer
    to a heatproof bowl. Cover surface with plastic wrap and
    place in fridge for 1 hour or until custard is cold.

2   Preheat oven to 200°C. Using an 8 cm round pastry cutter,
    cut 12 rounds from pastry, and discard trimmed pastry.
    Roll out each round to a 10 cm disc between two sheets
    of baking paper. Lightly spray a 12-hole (⅓-cup capacity)
    muffin tin with oil. Line holes with pastry discs. Spoon
    custard into pastry shells. Sprinkle with nutmeg. Bake for
    20 minutes or until pastry is golden and filling starts to
    brown. Set aside in tin for 5 minutes before transferring to
    a wire rack to cool. Serve warm or at room temperature.

Cook's tips

✱ **These tarts are best eaten on the**
   day of baking so the pastry is crisp.

✱ **Serve with fresh sliced strawberries.**

The WW Essential Guide to Healthy Eating

Greek yoghurt fudge pops

5 **4** **4** SmartPoints value per serve

PREP 10 MIN + OVERNIGHT FREEZING / **SERVES** 6

1 cup (240 g) 99% fat-free plain
  Greek yoghurt
¾ cup (185 ml) skim milk
½ cup (45 g) cocoa powder
¼ cup (90 g) honey

1 Place all ingredients in a blender. Process until smooth (you'll need to scrape down sides with a spatula several times).

2 Divide mixture among six ⅓-cup capacity popsicle moulds. Freeze overnight until firm. Serve.

Cook's tip

Add a few dashes of high quality peppermint extract to these pops for a chocolate–mint treat.

Baked rice puddings *with* cherries

6 **5** **5** SmartPoints value per serve

PREP 10 MIN / **COOK** 45 MIN + COOLING / **SERVES** 4

⅓ cup (75 g) medium-grain
white rice

2 cups (500 ml) skim milk

2 eggs

1 egg yolk

¼ cup (55 g) granulated stevia

2 teaspoons vanilla extract

12 morello cherries in syrup

1 Preheat oven to 180°C. Lightly spray four ¾-cup (185 ml) capacity ovenproof dishes with oil. Place dishes in a baking dish.

2 Place rice in a sieve and rinse under cold water until water runs clear.

3 Bring 2 cups (500 ml) water to the boil in a small saucepan over medium heat. Add rice and simmer for 8 minutes or until just tender. Drain and set aside to cool.

4 Whisk milk, eggs, egg yolk, stevia and vanilla extract in a large bowl until combined. Transfer to a jug. Spoon cooled rice evenly into prepared dishes. Pour over egg mixture. Using a fork, stir each pudding to distribute the rice.

5 Pour enough boiling water into baking dish to come halfway up the sides of the dishes. Bake for 30–35 minutes or until set and golden. Cool for 5 minutes. Serve puddings topped with cherries.

Cook's tips

* These puddings can be served warm or cold.

* Swap cherries with strawberries, if preferred.

Banana *and* passionfruit ice-cream

PREP 20 MIN + 3 HRS FREEZING / **SERVES** 6

4 frozen bananas

2 teaspoons lemon juice

500 g reduced-fat vanilla
   ice-cream

¼ cup (60 ml) canned
   passionfruit pulp

100 g strawberries, hulled

1 Process bananas and lemon juice in a food processor until smooth. Add ice-cream and process until combined. Transfer to a large bowl. Stir in passionfruit pulp.

2 Pour banana mixture into a 6-cup (1.5 litre) capacity freezer-proof dish. Cover with foil and freeze for 3 hours or until firm. Serve ice-cream in scoops topped with strawberries.

Cook's tip

You can freeze ripe bananas in snap-lock bags or an airtight container for up to 3 months. Alternatively, frozen bananas are readily available from major supermarkets. They are also handy for making cakes and muffins.

The WW Essential Guide to Healthy Eating

Caramel slice

 SmartPoints value per serve

PREP 15 MIN / **COOK** 20 MIN + 2 HRS 15 MIN COOLING / **SERVES** 18

1 cup (150 g) dried apricots
⅓ cup (50 g) plain flour
1 tablespoon cocoa powder
⅓ cup (25 g) shredded or
   desiccated coconut
2 tablespoons brown sugar
2 eggs, separated
1¼ cups (400 g) sweetened skim
   condensed milk
2 tablespoons golden syrup
120 g dark chocolate melts

1   Preheat oven to 180°C. Spray a 17 cm x 25 cm slice tin
    with oil and line with baking paper.

2   Process apricots in a food processor until finely chopped.
    Add flour, cocoa, coconut and sugar and pulse until
    combined.

3   Set egg yolks aside. Using electric beaters, beat egg
    whites in a bowl until soft peaks form. Fold in apricot
    mixture. Press mixture evenly over base of prepared tin.
    Bake for 10 minutes.

4   Meanwhile, combine condensed milk and golden syrup
    in a small saucepan over medium heat. Cook, stirring
    constantly, for 6–7 minutes or until mixture thickens
    slightly and becomes light golden. Cool for 2 minutes
    and stir in egg yolks.

5   Spread caramel mixture evenly over base. Reduce oven
    temperature to 160°C and bake for a further 10 minutes.
    Remove from oven, cool slightly, then refrigerate for
    2 hours or until firm.

6   Melt chocolate in a heatproof bowl over a saucepan
    of simmering water or following packet instructions.
    Pour melted chocolate over caramel mixture and smooth
    with a palette knife. Refrigerate for 15 minutes to set.

7   Using a hot sharp knife, cut into 18 pieces and serve.

Index

The WW Essential Guide to Healthy Eating

The WW Essential Guide to Healthy Eating

Conversion chart

Measuring cups and spoons may vary slightly from one country to another, but the difference is generally not enough to affect a recipe. All cup and spoon measures are level. One Australian metric measuring cup holds 250 ml (8 fl oz), one Australian tablespoon holds 20 ml (4 teaspoons) and one Australian metric teaspoon holds 5 ml. North America, New Zealand and the UK use a 15 ml (3-teaspoon) tablespoon.

LENGTH

METRIC	IMPERIAL
3 mm	⅛ inch
6 mm	¼ inch
1 cm	½ inch
2.5 cm	1 inch
5 cm	2 inches
18 cm	7 inches
20 cm	8 inches
23 cm	9 inches
25 cm	10 inches
30 cm	12 inches

LIQUID MEASURES

ONE AMERICAN PINT	ONE IMPERIAL PINT
500 ml (16 fl oz)	600 ml (20 fl oz)

CUP	METRIC	IMPERIAL
⅛ cup	30 ml	1 fl oz
¼ cup	60 ml	2 fl oz
⅓ cup	80 ml	2½ fl oz
½ cup	125 ml	4 fl oz
⅔ cup	160 ml	5 fl oz
¾ cup	180 ml	6 fl oz
1 cup	250 ml	8 fl oz
2 cups	500 ml	16 fl oz
2¼ cups	560 ml	20 fl oz
4 cups	1 litre	32 fl oz

OVEN TEMPERATURES

CELSIUS	FAHRENHEIT
100°C	200°F
120°C	250°F
150°C	300°F
160°C	325°F
180°C	350°F
200°C	400°F
220°C	425°F

CELSIUS	GAS MARK
110°C	¼
130°C	½
140°C	1
150°C	2
170°C	3
180°C	4
190°C	5
200°C	6
220°C	7
230°C	8
240°C	9
250°C	10

DRY MEASURES

The most accurate way to measure dry ingredients is to weigh them. However, if using a cup, add the ingredient loosely to the cup and level with a knife; don't compact the ingredient unless the recipe states 'firmly packed'.

METRIC	IMPERIAL
15 g	½ oz
30 g	1 oz
60 g	2 oz
125 g	4 oz (¼ lb)
185 g	6 oz
250 g	8 oz (½ lb)
375 g	12 oz (¾ lb)
500 g	16 oz (1 lb)
1 kg	32 oz (2 lb)

First published 2020 in Macmillan
by Pan Macmillan Australia Pty Limited
Level 25, 1 Market Street, Sydney, New South Wales
Australia 2000

A CIP catalogue record for this book is available from the National Library of Australia:
http://catalogue.nla.gov.au

Design by Northwood Green
Index by Helena Holmgren
Prop and food styling by Vanessa Austin
Food preparation by Sarah Mayoh
Colour + reproduction by Splitting Image Colour Studio
Printed in China by Imago Printing International Limited

10 9 8 7 6 5 4